Eleanor Stephens trained as a psychologist and counsellor specializing in women's health and sexuality. She is a writer and broadcaster who runs her own independent television production company, Stephens Kerr Ltd. Her books include *The Survivors' Guide* and *Compulsion,* and she is editor of the television series, 'Love Talk'.

Jonathan Bairstow is an artist and animator who studied at the Royal College of Art. His work has won several international awards.

Love
talk

A young person's guide
to SEX, LOVE and LIFE

Eleanor Stephens

With cartoons by
Jonathan Bairstow

Published by VIRAGO PRESS Limited 1991
20-23 Mandela Street
Camden Town,
London NW1 0HQ

A CIP Catalogue record for this book is available from the British Library

Designed and Typeset on Apple Mac by David Black
Printed in Great Britain by
The Guernsey Press Co Ltd, Channel Islands

for our mothers

many thanks

■ To Tim Robinson for his invaluble help on this book and to everyone who contributed to the SEX TALK and LOVE TALK television series, especially Charlotte Black.

■ To Stephen Garrett at Channel 4, Lennie Goodings at Virago and to my partner, Jean Kerr at Stephens Kerr.

■ To the staff of many organizations who put us right on the facts, especially The Family Planning Association and The Terrence Higgins Trust.

■ To Eliza Stephens and all the young people who contributed their wisdom, humour and inspiration for the series and this book.

CONTENTS

Getting the safer sex you want
Testing for HIV

Check ups and cancer screening
Alternative and complementary
Mental problems
Coping with illness and death
Drug use and abuse
Legal and illegal drugs
Getting off drugs
Getting what you want: assertiveness training

THIS BOOK IS ABOUT CHANGE AND CHOICE AND COMMUNICATION

Growing up involves coming to terms with **CHANGE** – changes to your body, your mind, and your feelings. The more you understand these changes, the better you will feel about yourself and the more you will appreciate what others are going through.

Being alive is also about **CHOICE** and making decisions which are right for you. The more information you have about the options, the more likely you are to make good choices, to learn from your mistakes and to take control of your own life.

Some of the most important changes and choices concern our development as sexual people capable of loving relationships. Establishing good relationships with others depends on loving and respecting ourselves first. **Love Talk** examines some of the pleasures and pitfalls of love and sex and how to survive them.

Along with change and choice goes **COMMUNICATION**. However confused or isolated you may feel, talking it over really does help. Throughout this book, we suggest places to go to find practical help and advice or just a sympathetic person to talk to. When a specific place is referred to, you'll see the symbol ⌂ These addresses and telephone numbers are listed at the back of the book.

BODY TALK

2

NO THANKS TO A BRA, I THINK THEY'RE SILLY.

BUT YOU DON'T HAVE TO BOUNCE AROUND PLAYING NETBALL IN FRONT OF COCKY TWELVE-YEAR OLDS. MY MUM MUST HAVE FORGOTTEN WHAT IT'S LIKE.

YEAH, WHY DON'T WE BUY HER ONE?

KNICKERBO
ET
SA
SA
SA

OH HI KIM! FANCY SEEING YOU HERE. WHAT ARE YOU GETTING?

I WAS THINKING OF GETTING A BODY!

OOOH! COULD YOU GET ME A NEW ONE? AND MAKE IT SKINNY!

chapter one

BODY TALK

Some of the most dramatic physical changes we ever experience take place between the ages of about ten and sixteen. This period of transition, known as puberty, carries us from childhood to maturity. It can be an exciting time but also an anxious one, particularly if you don't know what to expect.

Many of you reading this book will have gone through puberty already but don't skip to the next chapter. Sex education in Britain is not nearly as good as it should be. That's one of the reasons why the numbers of unwanted pregnancies here are on the increase and so much higher than in countries like Holland and Sweden. There, sex education begins at a much younger age and is far more open and explicit.

Many adults don't understand how their bodies work. Women in particular are still in the dark about what their sex organs look like and how they function. Lots of myths and so-called old wives' tales still abound so even if you think you know all this, take a quick look.

IT'S YOUR HORMONES

Changes at puberty are triggered by a tiny gland in our brains called the pituitary gland, which sends chemicals called hormones into the blood stream. These hormones travel to the sex glands (in girls the ovaries, in boys the testicles) and start them working.

These glands then produce hormones which set off all the changes in the rest of our bodies. Men and women have different hormones so whereas before puberty, girls' and boys' bodies look quite similar, afterwards they end up looking quite different.

We are all individuals and develop at our own rate. So, as Yvonne and Rosa realize, there's no fixed timetable of events. Some girls start their periods as young as nine, others as late as seventeen.

CHANGES WHICH AFFECT BOTH SEXES

■ Spurts in height and weight and development of muscles.

■ Growth of sex organs.

■ Deepening of voice (even in girls).

■ More active skin glands which may cause greasy skin and spots.

■ Development of new sweat glands.

■ Growth of underarm hair and pubic hair (between the legs). Arms and legs get hairier too.

CHANGES WHICH AFFECT GIRLS

■ Breasts develop and nipples stand out more. They may feel slightly painful as they grow.

■ Hips get rounder and waist thinner.

■ Sex organs develop and ovaries start to produce eggs which if fertilized by a sperm, can grow into a baby.

■ Later on in puberty, periods start. They may be irregular at first but will eventually settle down to a monthly cycle known as the menstrual cycle.

■ Girls may experience their first orgasm through masturbation.

CHANGES WHICH AFFECT BOYS

■ Penis and testicles grow larger and skin around the testicles becomes redder and coarser. Testicles start to produce sperm.

■ More frequent erections ('hard-ons') in which blood rushes to the penis, making it stiff. Boys experience their first ejaculation in which one or two tablespoons of creamy liquid called semen (or 'come', sometimes spelt 'cum') spurts out of the penis.

■ Chest and shoulders develop.
■ Later on in puberty, hair starts growing on face and may grow on chest.

SEX ORGANS

It's important to know what your sexual and reproductive organs look and feel like and to know the names for the different parts and how they work. So here's a brief guide to the bits that matter:

FEMALE

Men are used to handling their sex organs often but the female organs are tucked away and it's easy to ignore them. It's well worth taking some personal time with a mirror to check out the different parts. Either squat or sit on the edge of a chair in a brightly lit spot with your legs apart. Hold a mirror in one hand and use the other hand to explore. Don't feel shy or embarrassed about this part of your body. It belongs to you so get to know it. (It's also a great help knowing your way around if you want to use tampons for your period.)

Vulva This is the proper term for the whole area from the pubic mound to the entrance of the vagina. It's also called by slang names like 'fanny' and 'pussy'. You may choose your own pet name just as boys have affectionate names for their penis.

Lips of the vagina The vagina is rather like a mouth with two sets of lips or labia - the outer lips and the inner lips.

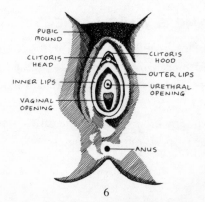

The outer lips are fatty and covered with hair. The inner lips are smaller, hairless and sensitive to touch. When you are turned on, they swell slightly and turn a darker colour. Vaginal lips can vary enormously in size and shape so don't worry if yours look different from ones you see in books or magazines.

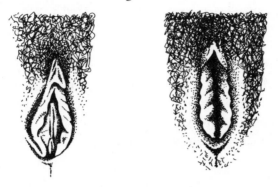

C l i t o r i s Below the pubic mound, where the inner lips meet, lies the clitoris. This is the most sensitive organ in the whole genital area. It's the female equivalent of the penis and has lots of nerve endings. In adults, it is about the size of a pea and becomes slightly bigger when you are sexually aroused.

To see your clitoris clearly, you may need to pull back the hood formed by the outer lips. Even then, you can only see the tip. If you press your fingers just above it, you will feel a ridge under the skin – this is the clitoral shaft. Many women find that the tip is too sensitive to press on and prefer pressure on the shaft. The stimulation of the clitoris (by direct or indirect pressure) is what eventually leads to an orgasm or sexual climax. (See Chapter 3.)

U r e t h r a This is a very small opening just below the clitoris through which urine passes when we pee. (Sometimes called the 'pee-hole'.) It's linked by a tube to the bladder which is like a bag in which the urine collects. Because the urethra is so close to the vagina, it may sometimes become sore after a lot of sexual stimulation. It usually recovers quickly unless you are unlucky enough to have an attack of the all too common urinary infection, cystitis. (See Chapter 13.)

Vagina The vaginal opening is just below the urethra and you'll have to use your fingers to find it. It's not a round hole but more like a fold between the inner labia. The vagina is inside the body and is quite small, only 75-127 mm (3-5 ins) long. But the folds of the wall of the vagina expand like a balloon. The vagina stretches easily to take a tampon, a man's erect penis and biggest of all, a baby on its way out through the vagina during birth.

The walls of the vagina are usually slightly wet. These juices or secretions (which taste slightly salty) keep the vagina clean and protect against infections. The amount of secretions vary according to where you are in your menstrual cycle and you will notice that the vagina gets wetter and well lubricated when you are sexually aroused.

Another word for the vagina is 'cunt'. This is a perfectly good Anglo-Saxon word but unfortunately it's more often used, usually by men, as a term of abuse. (Similar to using the slang word for penis, 'prick', as an insult.) However, it's also used between lovers as a term of affection or pride.

Cervix If you reach up inside your vagina as far as you can with your finger, angling it towards your back, you may be able to feel your cervix. It feels a bit like a small round chin with a dimple in it. The dimple is called the os and is the opening into the womb or uterus. Menstrual blood passes through this opening each month. During childbirth, the cervix expands to allow the baby to pass through but nothing can get up it by mistake, so don't worry about losing your tampon inside you!

Hymen The hymen is a thin skin or membrane which covers part of the vaginal opening. It used to be known as the 'maidenhead' and unbroken, was considered a sign that a girl was still a virgin and had never had sex with penetration. In some cultures, girls were examined before marriage to check whether the hymen was still in one piece. In fact, many girls have no visible hymen and it is easily stretched or torn by lots of activities other than sex: gymnastics, horse-riding or using a tampon, for example.

Breasts Also known as tits, boobs, bosoms or knockers, these develop dramatically during puberty. Breasts consist of fatty tissue and glands that produce milk after a baby is born. As the breasts develop, the nipples also get bigger and the skin around the nipples (the aureola) will get darker. Sometimes hairs grow around the nipples or between the breasts. If they worry you, it is safe to pluck them with tweezers. Almost all women worry about the size and shape of their breasts, rather as boys worry about the size of their penis. Fashions change too and encourage us to feel dissatisfied with our shape. (See Chapter 9 on body image.)

Whether your breasts are large or small makes absolutely no difference either to your ability to breast feed or to enjoy pleasurable sensations during lovemaking. Some women find their breasts are very responsive to being kissed and stroked, others find it pleasant but not particularly arousing. You may find that their sensitivity varies at different times of the month and that they can become quite tender – especially before your period. A well-fitted bra may help, but don't feel you have to wear a bra if you are comfortable without one.

MALE

Penis Also known as cock, prick, willy, dick and many other names. The penis, like the clitoris, consists of two parts: the tip or glans at the head and the longer shaft. The tip of the penis is very sensitive with thousands of nerve endings. Right in the centre is the opening of a tube called the urethra, which runs through the middle of the penis. This has two important functions: to carry urine and to carry sperm. The tube divides into two inside the body. One goes to the bladder and the other goes to the internal sex organs which produce sperm and semen.

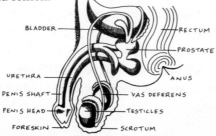

9

The penis is made of spongy tissue full of small blood vessels. During sexual arousal, or sometimes for no reason at all, the blood pumps into the penis and a muscle at the base of the penis tightens so that the blood cannot escape. This makes the penis grow bigger and harder, causing an erection or 'hard-on'. When the excitement dies down, whether or not you've had an orgasm, the muscles relax and the penis shrinks.

There is no standard shape or size of penis. They vary just as much as feet or noses vary from one person to another. The size of the limp penis is no indication of how big it will be when erect. This can be a cause of great concern to boys because the size of penis has become wrongly associated with being a good lover. (It's certainly not as simple as that!) The average size of an erect penis is about six inches: some are shorter and thicker, others longer and thinner.

During puberty, you may notice small pimples on the skin as the hair follicles grow. Pubic hair grows around the base of the penis and some hairs may grow on the penis itself. You may also notice quite prominent veins under the skin, especially when erect.

Foreskin All boys are born with a thickish fold of skin which covers the glans, similar to the hood which covers the clitoris. This foreskin can easily be drawn back over the shaft, which is what happens when the penis is erect. The foreskin can be cut off in a simple operation known as circumcision. Some people believe there are good hygienic reasons for doing this because it's easier to keep a circumcised penis clean. Jewish boys are circumcised a few days after birth and some cultures circumcise older boys. This operation makes absolutely no difference to sexual responsiveness.

Testicles Slang terms for testicles include balls, bollocks, nuts, cobblers. The two testicles are enclosed in a bag of crinkly skin known as the scrotum. At puberty, the testicles start producing the sex hormone which starts making sperm. The sperm are stored in lots of tiny tubes inside the balls and mix with seminal fluid produced in the prostate gland.

Semen and sperm Semen or seminal fluid (also known as spunk or come) is a thick, milky liquid which contains millions of sperm. When a boy has an orgasm, semen is pumped out of the penis in four or five short bursts. This is known as ejaculating or coming. Most boys start to ejaculate by the age of twelve, either through rubbing the penis while masturbating (or 'wanking') or while asleep in what's known as a 'wet dream'. If the boy ejaculates inside the girl's vagina during sex, the sperm, which are like microscopic tadpoles, can swim up through the vagina into the womb. If it's the time of the month when the female egg has been released, one of these sperm may fertilize the egg. This means that conception takes place and the woman becomes pregnant.

MALE AND FEMALE

Pubic hair One of the sure signs of puberty is the growth of hair around the outer sex organs. The hair will be soft and fine at first, becoming coarser and thicker, depending on the hair on the rest of your body. If you have thick curly hair on your head, your pubic hair will be similar. Blondes may have much less pubic hair and blond-haired boys may have little or no chest hair. The hair grows most thickly on the pubic mound and may stretch up in a thin line towards the belly button or navel. It grows between the legs right round to the anus.

Anus Another opening in this part of our body is the anus (often called 'arsehole') which is the exit point of the bowels. When the food we eat is broken down and digested, the solid leftovers (properly called 'faeces', pronounced 'feesees', but also known as excrement, shit or crap) travel through the bowels and pass out through the anus when we have a bowel movement. The anus is quite a sensitive organ and can also be a focus of sexual pleasure. (See Chapter 5 on safer sex.)

UNDERSTANDING PERIODS

Many people still grow up knowing little or nothing about menstruation and reproduction, with the result that these natural processes become shrouded in mystery and fear. It's important that both sexes understand as much as possible about each other's bodies, and there are excellent books which describe the processes in detail (see end of this chapter).

Boys often complain that it's hard for them to understand their girl friend's or their mother's moods because talking about periods is still such a taboo subject. Here are the answers to some questions which girls often ask and they are essential reading for males too:

What is a period? A period is the name given to the flow of menstrual blood, 'menstrual' meaning 'monthly'. This takes place roughly once a month and can last anything from two to seven days. The average period lasts five days. The amount of blood lost is actually very small (only a few tablespoons) and the flow is often heavier on the first few days and then trickles off. The blood, which is actually a mixture of blood and tissue, may start bright red and then become darker towards the end of your period.

What is the menstrual cycle? Menstrual means 'monthly' and the period of bleeding marks Phase One of this cycle. (So the first day of bleeding is Day One.) The bleeding is caused by the lining of the womb breaking down and being passed out of the body through the cervix and vagina.

In Phase Two (approximately Days Six to Thirteen) the pituitary gland in the brain produces hormones which tell the ovary to get ready to produce an egg and start the lining of the womb thickening again.

In Phase Three ovulation takes place and the egg is produced ('ova' means 'egg'). The ripe ovary produces one egg each month. We have two ovaries, right and left, and they take it in turns to produce the egg. Ovulation takes place about fourteen days before the next period. So for a woman with a regular twenty-eight-day cycle, ovulation will take place between Days Twelve and Sixteen. Unfortunately most women can't detect when they are ovulating, otherwise birth control would be a lot simpler.

During Phase Four of the cycle, the egg makes its way down the fallopian tubes towards the womb and its lining. The lining of the womb or uterus gets thicker to receive and feed the egg if it is fertilized. If a sperm meets the egg at this time, fertilization is very likely. But unless this happens, the egg disintegrates along with the lining which is no longer needed. It passes out of the body as menstrual blood on Day One of the next cycle. Then the whole process begins again!

Why haven't I started yet? Most girls start their periods between the ages of ten and fourteen but some are a bit earlier or later. The exact time you will start is dictated by your hormones and no one can tell you when that will be. Certain illnesses like the eating disorder, anorexia, can also prevent your periods from starting. If you are worried, talk to your doctor.

Why aren't my periods regular? The monthly, twenty-eight-day cycle is the *average* length of time from the beginning of one period to the beginning of the next. But your cycle may be as short as twenty-one days or as long as thirty-five days. (And the length of each period may vary from three or four days to six or seven.) Very few girls are completely regular, particularly during the first few years.

What is PMT and does everyone have it? PMT stands for 'pre-menstrual tension' and describes the feelings that some, but by no means all, women have, for a few days before their period starts. The symptoms are partly physical - a bloated, uncomfortable heaviness and tender breasts - and partly emotional - getting more irritable and moody than usual.

Certainly not everyone suffers from PMT. But if you do, it's better to tell your family or friends why you may snap their heads off at certain times of the month. Although there's been a lot of research into PMT in the last twenty years, it's still not fully understood and there is no magical cure. But if it's really bad, talk to your doctor.

What causes period pains and what cures them? Like PMT, not everyone suffers from cramps or stomach ache during their periods and no one really knows exactly what causes period pains. But most women do get some discomfort such as a dragging feeling in their belly or vagina. A few suffer really painful cramps for the first day or two. One theory is that the pains are caused by contractions of the womb as it pushes out the menstrual blood.

You may find that exercise helps or that having an orgasm relieves the congestion and cramps. Or you may prefer to curl up with a hot water bottle and a hot drink. Painkillers will also help but if the pain is really severe, check with your doctor that nothing else is wrong.

However, it's a mistake to assume that a period has to be a 'curse' as it used to be called. In fact, some women feel extra energetic and extra sexual during their period. We all react differently and our responses change throughout our lives.

Is it OK to have sex during your period? It's fine to have sex during a period and to bathe, wash your hair, play sport, etc. In fact, some girls find they feel more physical at this time. But penetrative sex can be a bit messy and some people prefer not to have penetration for the first couple of days when the blood flow is heavier. Above all, do not believe the myth that you can't get pregnant during a period. You can, so be sure to use your usual birth control method. (See Chapter 6.)

What is the menopause? The menopause is another stage of a woman's life cycle rather like puberty. Just as chemical messengers (hormones) start off the whole process of menstruation and reproduction, so hormonal changes at the menopause stop the ovaries producing eggs. This means pregnancy cannot take place and so periods stop too. This change, as it's known, can happen at any age between the mid forties and mid fifties, or earlier as a result of illness or surgery. Just like puberty, it's a period of adjustment and it may cause some difficulties for a while. So it's good to be understanding if your mother or a friend is going through the menopause.

Do men have a cycle too? Men don't have a monthly cycle like women but they are affected by hormonal changes and this can cause moods and emotional upheavals too, especially at puberty (see next chapter). Recently it's become common to talk about men experiencing a 'mid life crisis' rather as women go through the menopause. This is probably more psychological than physical.

TO FIND OUT MORE

What's Happening To My Body? A Growing Up Guide For Parents and Daughters and *A Growing Up Guide For Parents and Sons.* Both books are by Linda Madaras and published by Penguin.
Our Bodies, Ourselves, Angela Phillips and Jill Rakusen, published by Penguin.

MIND TALK

16

MIND TALK

The physical changes which are part of puberty don't just affect our bodies. They affect our minds and our feelings too. Very few of us get through adolescence without suffering doubt and insecurity about ourselves and our relationships with others. This process can be described as a quest for identity – a journey to find out who you are.

This quest continues throughout life, but the years after puberty are a particularly intense time of self-exploration. And it's not all bad! As well as the insecurities, there's the freedom of greater independence, the excitement of discovering the new you and the pleasures of friendship and love.

HOW DO I LOOK?

Worrying about how you look and feeling bad about your body is one of the most common sources of insecurity. Of course, the worries often go deeper than that but it's easy to project them onto the size of your nose or whether your breasts are too small.

I remember talking with a group of women, all of us in our early twenties, about the size and shape of our breasts. Not a single one of us was content: too small, too big, too saggy, one bigger than the other, nipples too big, too small, too hairy... the list of complaints was endless. It was as though we were all part of a conspiracy to feel bad about ourselves. Realizing that everyone is dissatisfied makes you feel less of a freak.

The size and shape of willies, bottoms, noses, ears, legs, even feet, our height and our weight – these can all be sources of agony! We constantly compare ourselves to our friends, to people we admire and to images in films or magazines. Of course, we're bound to find we don't measure up and our self-esteem takes another knock. (See Chapter 9 for more on body image.)

As well as rejecting these false standards of perfection, it's worth remembering that your body is still changing and that bits that you hate now, you may value more later on. I hated being the tallest in the class when I was in school uniform - I used to be called Olive Oyl, after Popeye's beanpole girlfriend! But once I started buying my own clothes and stopped worrying about finding boys taller than me, I really enjoyed being tall.

Some of these worries can develop into consuming obsessions, and the problem becomes magnified out of all proportion - like Danny spending hours in the bathroom examining his spots! What may seem like a major disaster to you (a few spots or gaining a couple of pounds) may be hardly noticeable to someone else.

NO ONE UNDERSTANDS ME !

It's also easy to feel that other people aren't taking you or your problem seriously. This feeling of being ignored and misunderstood is a common complaint among young people. It turns into a vicious circle: because you are sure no one will understand how you feel, you don't try to communicate your feelings. But rather than storming off as Danny did, it may be more constructive to try to talk to someone about it. Parents have been young themselves and may understand better than you think. Or try talking to a friend. The cliché 'A problem shared is a problem halved' contains a lot of truth.

WILL ANYONE LIKE ME?

Another source of worry is how to form friendships and how to find a boy or girlfriend. This often boils down to the question: Am I a likeable or loveable person myself? Sometimes our self-confidence and sense of self-worth can hit rock bottom and we feel that no one could ever love us. This paranoid feeling can be self-fulfilling because if we don't value ourselves, how can we expect another person to value us? And how can we trust them if they say they do?

These are complex issues that will recur throughout our lives and no one can give you a recipe for good relationships. But research shows that certain personality qualities are more likely to get a positive response from people. They include:

A sense of humour Most people put this top of the list, way above looks, money, status, etc. Try not to take yourself or life too seriously all the time - even the heaviest situation can have its funny side if you look for it.

Taking an interest in others When you are in a group of people feeling tongue-tied and shy and wishing you weren't wearing that orange sweater, try to focus on someone else and ask them about themselves. They are probably feeling much the same as you, however confident they seem.

Knowing when to shut up and be a good listener When you are nervous, it's easy to talk too much and become a show-off or a bore. It's often better to ask questions and listen hard. Most people love talking about themselves. A good listener is just as popular as a brilliant conversationalist.

Having realistic expectations A friend once told me that his recipe for happiness was to have low expectations and a positive attitude. There's a lot of truth in this. Sometimes you can raise your hopes so high about a prospective event or person that you are bound to be disappointed. It's better to keep an open mind and see how things develop. Similarly, if you have a negative outlook, then you can usually find aspects of the person or situation which reinforce your negative viewpoint. So think positive!

'Do as you would be done by' This cliché has a lot going for it. If you like people to be friendly and warm towards you, then act in the same way to them. If you like people to keep their word and to be reliable and trustworthy, then act in the same way yourself. Good relationships thrive on equality, sharing and trust and are destroyed by double standards, dishonesty or one person exerting power over another. This is an important guide in a sexual relationship – for no one likes a selfish or insensitive lover.

ALL IN THE FAMILY

Many of the worst arguments and bad feeling centre around family life, and Danny's storming out of the house is a typical scenario. There's nothing new in this. Young people have always rowed with their parents. It's all part of the process of separating yourself from the family group on which you've been dependent since birth.

This desire to be independent is natural and healthy but it can be traumatic for both sides. It's hard for parents to come to terms with the fact that their precious baby is old enough to lead its own life. It's understandable that they worry about the young person's safety and happiness. But of course, their children have to have the freedom to make their own choices and their own mistakes just as they did. There's also more than a touch of jealousy involved – having a teenage child really brings it home to parents that they're not twenty-one any more themselves.

It may cheer you up to know that the arguments families have are often very similar and revolve around the same range of issues. See if these common parental sayings ring some bells:

- Staying out late: *'What time do you call this?'*
- Clothes, appearance and personal hygiene: *'What do you think you look like?'*
- Friends in general and boy/girlfriends in particular: *'I can't imagine what you see in him!'*
- Parties and holidays: *'Are their parents away?'*
- Untidiness and housework: *'You treat this place like a hotel!'*
- Money: *'You think money grows on trees!'*
- Studying, jobs and careers: *'What about your future?'*

COMMUNICATE

The first step to avoiding a row is to communicate. If you can discuss something before it becomes an argument, then there's the possibility of seeing each other's point of view and reaching a compromise. Once the sparks fly, reason goes out the window and you end up fighting to defend your position rather than to reach a solution.

For example, if Danny hadn't been so uptight about his appearance and had come downstairs earlier, he could have explained to his mum that he didn't want to eat a fried meal. Instead, his parents saw his lateness and criticism of the meal as an insult and rejection. (Food is often a symbol of love within families.) His sister, a rival for parental attention, exploits Danny's sensitivity and sure enough, Danny loses his temper and storms off. Of course, it's easy to analyse this when you're outside the situation - much harder when it's your feelings involved.

THE EMOTIONAL ROLLER COASTER

A certain amount of mood swings and emotional highs and lows are a result of physical and hormonal changes. On top of this are the practical problems that many young people face - no money, no job, rows with parents, nowhere to live, etc. These can all be good reasons for feeling depressed sometimes. And knowing that these dark moods will pass doesn't make it any easier to bear while you are going through them.

But some young people can hit long periods of depression and anxiety and may need expert help. If you find yourself constantly lethargic, depressed and lonely, depending too much on alcohol or drugs, often losing your temper, bursting into tears or feeling suicidal, then seek help. Go to your GP and ask for counselling. Your school or college may be able to refer you to a counsellor. Several organizations provide help specifically for young people and the Samaritans run a twenty-four hour nationwide telephone counselling service. ▲

If you feel you need help, don't let anyone brush you off just because of your age. Chronic depression and other kinds of mental illness can occur at any age and they can be treated. (See Chapter 11 on health.) The numbers of suicides among young people are rising so don't wait until you hit rock bottom. These years are crucial and should provide a chance to explore and experiment before you have too many responsibilities.

SEX TALK

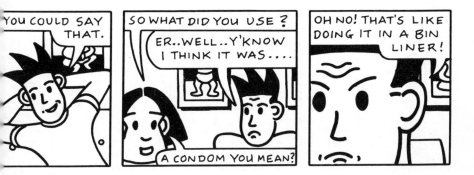

chapter three

SEX TALK

Sex may be the most natural thing in the world but that doesn't mean that we automatically know what to do with our bodies and the bodies of our partners. Sexual desire and the ability to be sexually aroused already exist in everyone but knowing how to trigger them off and enjoy them to the full has to be learned.

Partly because sex is often referred to as being 'natural', people feel that there is something wrong with them if they don't instinctively know how to make love. This is nonsense. The best lovers are those who understand their own sexual responses and are confident enough to share this knowledge with a partner at the same time as discovering what their partner enjoys. In other words, it's about exploration and communication – not just heaving away and hoping for the best!

EXPLORING OUR SEXUALITY

You may feel that you don't want to be sexual at the moment, but if you do, a good way to understand your sexual responses is to start off with your own body. That involves self-exploration and learning how to give yourself sexual pleasure. Free from any performance pressures, you can gradually discover more about your sexuality. We are all individuals with unique patterns of sexual enjoyment and these patterns will change as we grow older.

Masturbation can teach us about the kinds of stimulation our bodies enjoy and the variety of ways of experiencing pleasure. And by exploring different sexual fantasies, we can discover the kinds of things that turn us on. Then we can share some of these secrets of our sexuality with our lover, if we choose to.

Masturbation isn't just a substitute for sex with a partner. For most people, it's pleasurable in its own right and it's an excellent method of relaxation and stress relief. It's a much better way of providing a good night's sleep than alcohol or a sleeping pill. So why does masturbation have such a bad press that the slang word for it ('wanking') is used as an insult?

MASTURBATION: MYTHS AND TABOOS

There are lots of reasons, none of them good, why some people despise masturbation:

'It's disgusting!' Some people have inherited strong religious and traditional beliefs which view sex as a shameful activity. In their eyes, sexual activity is only justified if you are trying for a baby. Obviously, masturbation is not connected with reproduction so it is frowned on, together with other activities in which sexual pleasure is enjoyed for its own sake.

'It will make you blind!' People with these prejudices may even suggest that masturbation does you physical harm. Most of us have heard stories that it can make you blind, drive you insane, make you sterile, affect the shape of your sex organs, etc. There is absolutely no medical evidence for any of this. You may decide that masturbation isn't something you want to do but it certainly won't do you any harm.

'I don't need to masturbate because I've got a lover!' This kind of statement implies that only unattractive, lonely or sexually inadequate people like to masturbate. In fact, most people enjoy it and it can contribute to exciting and safe sex with a partner. Even if you are in a sexual relationship, it is quite normal to enjoy youself sexually on your own sometimes. You may have fantasies while masturbating that you don't want to have when you are making love with a partner.

'Only boys masturbate!' Masturbation is one of the ways boys learn about their bodies. They are usually quite open about it and some even have wanking competitions! So it's often assumed that only boys masturbate and this can make girls feel doubly guilty about their pleasure. In fact, most women masturbate even though they may be too shy to talk about it or they may not discover it until they are in their twenties or later. For both sexes, it's an excellent way to discover exactly the kind of stimulation you need to reach orgasm.

HOW TO MASTURBATE

Women's and men's genitals may look completely different but there are more similarities than meet the eye. Both men and women generally masturbate by stimulating the sexual organ which becomes erect during sexual arousal: the clitoris for women, the penis for men. As well as touching these organs, you may enjoy stroking other parts of your body too. And sex is never just in the genitals, it's also in the mind. So try out different sexual fantasies to enhance your pleasure.

Masturbation is not a race or an endurance test. Some people come in a few seconds and some people take up to an hour. It often depends on your mood. Just keep in mind that there is no 'normal' time, and that if you're not used to masturbating, it might take a little longer at first.

WOMEN MASTURBATING

Despite what a lot of men think, the vagina is not the main source of an orgasm. It's the clitoris which has the most nerve endings and it is regular and rhythmic stimulation of the clitoris which triggers off the orgasm reflex. For most women, directly stimulating the clitoris is necessary although others find it's too sensitive for direct pressure and prefer touching above and around it. Find out what's the best method for you. Get to know your body so later on you can share this with your lover.

There are lots of different masturbation methods to try. If possible, give yourself an hour in privacy in your bedroom or bathroom. Set the scene with some favourite music, candles or a bubble bath.

■ Before you begin, make friends with your body. You might enjoy looking at yourself naked in the mirror and rubbing your hands up and down your body. Discover your own sexy bits (known as 'erogenous zones') such as nipples or buttocks.

■ Rub a finger or several fingers over your clitoris, gradually increasing the speed of the movement. Experiment with different pressures and different speeds. Generally, women prefer faster and firmer strokes as they get closer to a climax.

■ Use your hand to press firmly down on your pubic mound and the whole genital area. Again, experiment with pressure and speed.

■ Put a sheet or a pillow between your legs and rub it backwards and forwards over your clitoris.

■ Insert a finger or two up your vagina or anus (bum) when you are about to come - it can make the feeling more intense.

■ Try a sex toy like a vibrator, either battery powered or mains. This will give you stronger and more regular stimulation than your fingers and is often the way women have their first orgasms.

■ Experiment with different positions: on your back perhaps, with a cushion under your hips, on your stomach, kneeling or any way that you fancy.

■ Fantasy can certainly increase your pleasure. You can weave your own erotic tales or look to literature for inspiration. Let your imagination run wild and don't feel guilty about the content. Most women fantasize and their fantasies cover a huge diversity of topics, as you can see from a book on this subject called *My Secret Garden*.

MEN MASTURBATING

Masturbation seems to be more straightforward for men, but there are still several ways to do it:

■ Make a fist, hold your penis quite firmly in it and jerk the hand up and down with a shaking action that gets quicker and quicker as you get closer to coming.

■ If you've got a foreskin (i.e. you haven't been circumcised) pull it backwards and forwards over the head of your penis.

■ Lie on your stomach and rub your body up and down on the sheets. You might enjoy coming this way without touching your penis with your hands.

■ Rub baby oil over your penis for increased sensation and try inserting a finger or two into your anus and moving it around.

■ Men enjoy fantasy too and this can certainly add to the excitement, whether it's a fantasy about someone you know or an imaginary partner. Some men get turned on by 'sexy pictures' in books or magazines. Understandably, many women dislike the way that women are portrayed in 'porno mags' so don't expect real life women to enjoy being humiliated in that way.

WHAT IS AN ORGASM?

Other words for orgasm include sexual peak or climax as well as 'coming'. People's personal descriptions of their orgasm vary wildly: an overwhelming wave of pleasure, an electric shock, a mild tingling sensation, sparks flying, teeth tingling, a gentle sigh. Orgasms feel different to different people and different to the same person at different times. However, an orgasm is a physical reflex like a sneeze and there is a definite sequence of events which always has to occur before someone reaches orgasm. There are four stages: excitement, plateau, climax and resolution:

E x c i t e m e n t In the first stage, the person will breathe more heavily, as heart rate and blood pressure increase. Blood rushes to most women's and some men's nipples, and to sexual organs. The clitoris or penis expands and the penis becomes erect. The clitoris also gets slightly bigger. The woman's vagina becomes wet and opens up inside. The man's balls swell slightly and draw up close to his body.

P l a t e a u This stage comes just before orgasm. Women's breasts get even bigger, as does the penis. Hot flushes, sweating and panting may occur and the body will start moving more and more jerkily as muscle tension increases. The inner vaginal lips and the entrance of the vagina swell while the man's semen moves from his testicles to the base of his penis. At this point, unless the stimulation suddenly stops, men and women are ready to come.

O r g a s m *Male:* When a man ejaculates, the sperm comes rushing out along the tube of his penis and spurts out of the tip in four or five spasms. The spasms spread to all his sex organs, his anus and sometimes the whole of his body. Once his orgasm is over, he usually has to wait at least ten minutes or longer before he can get another erection.

Female: The woman's orgasm involves a series of short rhythmical spasms in the walls of the outer part of the vagina. These spasms spread up to the womb, and like the man, to all the sex organs and sometimes the whole body. Some women can come over and over again if they continue to be stimulated and they may feel dissatisfied if their partner stops immediately after the first orgasm.

R e s o l u t i o n After orgasm, the blood gradually leaves the sexual organs. Blood pressure and breathing rate will return to normal. There is a delicious feeling of relaxation and well-being, sometimes known as 'afterglow', and it's a good time to cuddle and share the closeness and affection of being lovers. Some people, especially men, fall asleep straight after coming and this can make their partner feel neglected. Others feel full of energy and are revitalized.

LOVE AND BLISS

Making love isn't about clocking up orgasms and there are no points to be scored. It's about sharing an intimate part of yourself with someone you trust. You can enjoy lots of sensual and sexual pleasure without having orgasms, so don't feel you have to climax every time you get turned on. (And don't believe any boy who tells you his balls will go blue if he doesn't climax!) Some girls feel pressurized into faking orgasms to boost their partner's ego. This is a foolish idea and can store up many problems for the future. So try to be true to yourself and trust your partner enough to explain what you enjoy and what you want to give and receive. Communication is the key - even the closest of lovers aren't telepathic!

TO FIND OUT MORE

My Secret Garden, Nancy Friday, published by Quartet.

♥ ♥ ♥ ♥ ♥

THE FIRST TIME

chapter four

THE FIRST TIME

Virginity used to be prized as a virtue and it was assumed that girls would remain virgins until they married. Young men, on the other hand, were expected to have some pre-marital experience in order to initiate their brides. Although sexual morality has changed and the majority of couples make love before marriage, double standards about boys' and girls' sexual roles still exist. A boy becomes a man when he loses his virginity but a girl may become a 'slag' when she does the same.

These ideas are less powerful than they were and many teenagers of both sexes feel a lot of pressure to lose their virginity. They worry that they aren't streetwise, sophisticated or adult unless they've had sex. As a result, many people embark on their first sexual experience before they are really ready. Others, who feel embarrassed by their lack of sexual experience, pretend that they've had sex. Then when it comes to the first time, they feel nervous because they've led their partner to believe that they have knowledge and confidence which they really lack.

Even if you are ready for your first sexual experience and it's with someone you love and fancy, sex is often a bit of a let-down the first few times, particularly if you are expecting the earth to move. Sex is something you have to learn to enjoy to the full, so the first time you make love, it's almost bound to be disappointing.

The best approach is to relax about the whole thing and take it slowly. You're likely to be making love for the next fifty years, so there's no big rush. There's nothing cool or sophisticated about painful or embarrassing fumbling and sadly, this tends to be most people's memory of their first sexual encounter. Wait until you meet someone you love and trust and chose the time that's right for you both.

ARE YOU READY FOR LOVE?

Lots of young people want the first time they have sex to be with someone they love. The problem is recognizing what love is: many young people will think that they are in love, yet not long afterwards they'll be laughing to think that they thought that was true love. Love can come in many guises and other feelings can be confused with love. Here are some points to consider:

Love or infatuation? It is very common in your teens (and later) to become infatuated with or have a 'crush' on someone you know. It is also very common to feel that this must be love, particularly as the emotions can feel quite overwhelming. However, there are differences between love and infatuation. With an infatuation, you often hardly know the person and adore him or her from a distance. Your feelings are based on your own needs and your own fantasies. This fantasy often evaporates once you get to know the object of your passion.

On the other hand, when you fall in love, although you often romanticize the person you're falling in love with, your love increases as you get to know them. In this case, your feelings are based on reality and knowledge, not fiction.

36

Loving and falling in love People often get confused by the different kinds of love they can feel. You can love your mother or your cat, but those emotions are often steady emotions that you may not even be aware of feeling. Falling in love, however, can dominate your life for a while and you are constantly aware of feeling high and walking on air, or plunged to the depths of despair.

In most relationships, the crazy euphoria of being in love is gradually replaced by a more stable, more lasting but perhaps less exciting feeling of love. Some people become so hooked on the excitement of being in love that they never reach the second stage at all.

One way to fall in love? As with having sex, there are many ways to fall in love. Some people seem to go slightly mad, staying up all night writing poems about their beloved. They think about this person all the time and shower them with presents. Others may be a lot more relaxed about their emotions and much less obviously overwhelmed by them. This doesn't mean that their feelings are superficial. In fact, sometimes the very dramatic lovers are in love with the drama itself and are most likely to betray their partner as soon as the excitement has worn off. The quieter lovers may well turn out to be more constant and to love more generously.

EXPRESSING YOUR LOVE

Whenever it happens, falling in love is usually a thrilling emotion and greatly adds to the pleasure and intensity of life. And saying 'I love you' for the first time can also be exciting, particularly when it's reciprocated. But it's not always as simple as it sounds. If you are agonizing over whether or not to say those three magic words, here are some some considerations:

Afraid that your love may not be returned? If you're sure you're in love with your partner, you still might find it difficult to say so because you're worried about putting your partner off. But if your partner is scared by what you say, and doesn't feel the same, you need to know this. It's probably better in the long run not to hide your feelings.

Desperate to be in love? Some people fall in love with almost anyone they're going out with, because they want the security of a committed relationship. If you find yourself continually falling in love very quickly, then it might be best to try to hold yourself back. Wait a while and see if you really are in love with your partner. Think about whether you and your partner really hit it off before you declare your love.

Out for the thrills? If you're the kind of person who falls very easily in and then out of love, you should be careful about hurting your partner's feelings. You may confess undying love, raise the emotional stakes and then let them down. Try to avoid playing with people's emotions in this way and be alert to the kind of person who might do this to you.

Love or sex? It's very easy to tell people that you love them just because you really fancy them like mad. Some girls, in particular, convince themselves they must be in love because they feel guilty about these sexual feelings. As people get older they tend to realize that sexual attraction can be mistaken for love and some couples even agree not to hold each other to vows or commitments exchanged at the height of passion. So avoid saying things you don't mean in the heat of the moment and don't take other people's expressions of love too seriously if they're confined to the bedroom.

Ultimately, what really counts is whether or not people show their love by caring for each other consistently. What you and your partner do rather than say is the real test of that love.

ARE YOU AND YOUR PARTNER READY FOR SEX?

Before rushing into bed or onto the back seat of the car, ask yourself these questions:

■ While sex can be a pleasurable experience for its own sake, it's a thousand times better with someone you love and trust. Communication and shared intimacy is an essential ingredient of good lovemaking and this can be difficult to achieve with someone you've just met or don't know well, however much you fancy them. Do you feel close enough to the person to want to share this intimacy?

■ Do you really desire sex now, or are you mostly wanting it because of social pressure, or pressure from your girl/boyfriend? You can have a close physical relationship with someone without needing to have sex, so if that's what you want, stick to it.

■ Sex, particularly the first time, might well make you feel exposed and vulnerable. After all, it's one of the most intimate things we ever do. Are you ready to handle these feelings? Do you trust your partner enough to open yourself up in this way?

■ Sex can cause all sorts of emotional upheavals and it's easy for either of you to get hurt. If you aren't in love with your partner, you may find yourself falling in love because of the vulnerability you feel after sex. Are you ready for the greater intensity and commitment this will involve? And how will you cope with rejection if your partner reacts differently?

■ If you are not sure you want to make love but go ahead anyway, you may feel very guilty afterwards. This may cause you to resent your partner and spoil the relationship. Or you may convince yourself you are in love in order to justify your decision. Either way, you are creating problems for yourself – so don't be frightened to admit you've made a mistake and wait until you feel the time is right.

■ Are you sorted out about safer sex and contraception? Yes, you can get pregnant or catch an infection The First Time! (See Chapter 5 on safer sex and Chapter 13 on sexually transmitted diseases.)

If you've thought these things through and still want to go ahead, you must also think about your partner's feelings. Ask yourself whether they really feel the same or are just agreeing to please you. Pressurizing someone to have sex when they aren't certain they want to, shows a lack of respect for their feelings and means you probably won't enjoy the experience much either. Good lovemaking needs two enthusiastic and willing partners.

MAKE THE FIRST TIME THE RIGHT TIME

A lot of this may seem plain common sense but many people rush into sexual relationships without ever thinking out these issues. In fact, lots of people first have sex when they're drunk or at a party with someone they hardly know. They don't think about their partner's feelings or about contraception or guarding against AIDS. No wonder the whole thing is often a bit of a disaster!

Once you have decided that you are ready for a sexual relationship, keep these points in mind:

Make it safe Protect yourself against unwanted pregnancy and unless you're absolutely sure that both of you are virgins who have never injected drugs, protect against the HIV virus which causes AIDS. Don't move a muscle until you've thought about these things. (See Chapter 5 about safer sex and Chapter 6 about birth control.)

Nerves are normal Almost everyone feels nervous and it's better to admit this to your partner. Nerves can cause certain problems which will sort themselves out in time. A man may find that he can't get or maintain an erection because he's worrying too much about it. He might find, on the other hand, that he comes far too quickly. A woman might find that her vaginal juices dry up and it may be painful for her partner to put his fingers or penis inside her. (See Chapter 12 for more about these problems.)

Don't expect too much If you think of sex as something that gets better with practice then see the first time as a stepping stone to greater pleasure. Usually it takes a few years of sexual activity before someone reaches their full sexual potential.

Sex doesn't just mean penetration A lot of people don't feel that they've really 'done it' unless a penis has gone up into a 'hole'. All sexual acts other than penetration are sometimes dismissed as 'heavy petting' or 'foreplay', as if they are lesser forms of pleasure whose only point is to build up to the 'real thing'.

Some people think that you only lose your virginity if you 'screw'. This would mean, logically, that lesbians who never have penetrative sex with a man never lose their virginity! There are lots of different things you can do which don't involve penetration and which both you and your partner might prefer. (See Chapter 5 for the list of 'low risk' and 'no risk' activities which are fun and don't involve penetration.)

Women count too! Because so many people think that sex equals penetration, that's often all that happens when a couple first have sex. (This is sometimes described as 'Wham, bam, thank you ma'am!') This can be a real let-down for the girl since it's direct or indirect clitoral stimulation which leads to full sexual arousal and orgasm. (See Chapter 3.)

So sexual partners should think about using their fingers and tongues to help a woman climax if she wants to. Women should feel self-confident about touching themselves during or after penetration if they wish. It leaves their partner's hands free to explore other erogenous zones too. Alternatively, they should feel confident about guiding their partner's hand in the right direction and showing him or her how to please them. All this takes trust and time and isn't likely to happen if you're drunk at a party!

Men don't have to be studs A lot of boys feel that they have to prove themselves as 'good lovers' straight away. This usually means pretending to know what you're doing when you don't and, in heterosexual relationships, generally trying to make all the sexual decisions for the couple. In reality, a woman is far more likely to be impressed if you drop that act, show vulnerability and ask her what she wants you to do.

Celibacy can be fun too! Believe it or not, lots of people lead very happy and full lives without sex. (This is known as being celibate.) You may be one of them. Talking, kissing, and cuddling are all ways of expressing love and intimacy and this doesn't have to lead to sexual intercourse.

Keep a sense of humour This is crucial. Some people say that God invented sex as a joke on humans! So never be afraid to laugh about it.

chapter five

SAFE LOVING

Love and sex can provide some of life's greatest joys as well as numerous pitfalls and challenges. Apart from the emotional problems that can arise, making love without taking precautions can lead to unwanted pregnancy as well as the fatal illness, AIDS.

AIDS can affect anybody, gay or straight, and everyone who is having an active sex life should take steps to protect themselves. This doesn't mean that sex isn't just as exciting. What's important is being relaxed enough to enjoy sex with the confidence that you are as safe as possible. Sex is a great source of pleasure and an expression of love, but it isn't worth dying for.

WHAT IS AIDS AND HIV?

AIDS stands for Acquired Immune Deficiency Syndrome. It's a disorder of the blood which means that a person's immune system stops working properly. People with AIDS get illnesses which they would normally overcome and these illnesses can eventually kill them.

AIDS is caused by HIV, the Human Immunodeficiency Virus, which attacks the immune system. Once someone contracts HIV, it will stay in their bloodstream for life. It may be several years before they show any symptoms but they can still pass on the virus to others.

HIV is present in the body fluids of an HIV infected person. That means that the virus is present in their blood, semen and possibly saliva. If the body fluids of a person with HIV come into contact with the body fluids of an uninfected person, the virus can be passed on. For instance, if a man with HIV ejaculates (comes) inside a woman's vagina and there is nothing to stop his semen from touching a small cut inside her vagina, then the virus can pass into her bloodstream. She will then become infected with HIV which means that she is then likely to develop AIDS at some time in the future. The illnesses related to AIDS will probably kill her eventually and could kill her baby should she become pregnant.

This sounds very grim indeed but now that AIDS has been known about for ten years or so, we should all know how to protect ourselves from catching the virus. It's called PRACTISING SAFER SEX.

It's also been established that the virus can't be passed on by everyday physical contact like hugging, shaking hands, drinking from the same cup, using the same telephone or musical instrument or toilet, or sharing a bath or swimming pool. However, drug users who share needles are definitely at risk because infected blood from one person can go straight into another's bloodstream.

WHAT IS SAFER SEX?

To prevent yourself from getting AIDS, you must stop yourself from becoming infected with HIV by practising safer sex. This means always using a condom unless you are absolutely sure that your partner doesn't have the HIV antibodies in their system. (People with the virus are called HIV positive because they show a positive result to the HIV antibody test.)

It is impossible to tell if your partner has HIV just by looking. Most people with the virus are healthy for years before they develop AIDS, but they can still pass it on. It can also be dangerous to trust what people say about their sexual history. Shame and embarrassment may stop them from being honest or they may simply not realize the risks. For instance, your boyfriend might have had sex with someone else before he met you. The person he had sex with might have had the virus without knowing it and passed it on to him. So unless you protect yourself, you could get the virus too.

So if you are in any doubt about whether you or your partner is HIV positive, you should always have safer sex. In fact, it's safer to assume that everyone has the virus and always to protect yourself.

KNOWING THE RISKS

AIDS has existed for at least ten years and some sexual acts have been found to be much more dangerous than others. The Terrence Higgins Trust, an organization which educates people about AIDS, puts sexual acts in three groups, according to how much chance there is of them giving a person the virus. These three groups of activities are called 'high risk', 'low risk', and 'no risk'.

HIGH RISK

Unprotected vaginal or anal intercourse

If a man puts his penis inside his lover's vagina or anus (bum) without first putting on a condom, his semen will come into direct contact with any tiny cuts or tears in the skin surrounding the vagina or anus. This is by far the most likely way to pass on the virus which leads to AIDS. (Unprotected vaginal intercourse can also lead to the woman becoming pregnant.) By the way, a man does not have to have an orgasm for the woman to risk getting the virus or becoming pregnant. Even if the man withdraws before he comes, some seminal fluid is often released before orgasm.

LOW RISK

These acts are very unlikely to lead to anyone getting HIV or becoming pregnant but there is still a very small risk.

Protected vaginal or anal intercourse

If you and your partner are protected by putting on a condom, it is very unlikely that the virus can be spread. However, condoms can split or have holes in them so you should always use a lubricant. The lubricant will enable the penis to slide in and out more easily and prevent the condom from tearing. The lubricant should be water-based, otherwise it might eat away at the rubber. It should also contain a spermicide which helps to kill any sperm and HIV which might escape.

Oral sex When you lick or suck your partner's penis or clitoris and vagina, some of their body fluids will come into contact with your mouth. If you have cuts or sores in your mouth it is possible, in theory, for the virus to get into your bloodstream. This is very unlikely indeed, even if a man comes inside his partner's mouth, because there are chemicals in saliva and in the stomach which kill the virus. To be absolutely safe, some people use flavoured condoms for oral sex. (You can buy them in a variety of flavours including banana, orange and strawberry!)

Deep or french kissing This involves opening your lips and letting your tongue play with the teeth, tongue and inside of your partner's mouth. This is a very, very unlikely way for the virus to spread.

NO RISK

There is absolutely no risk of you or your partner getting HIV or becoming pregnant if you enjoy these activities:

Mutual masturbation This means exciting yourself and your partner in two different ways: by rubbing and stroking your partner's genitals while they do the same to you, or by both of you stimulating yourselves at the same time. The second method can be more fun since everyone knows their own body best. If you try the first way, remember that all bodies are different: tell your partner what gives you pleasure and listen to what they say they enjoy. (Masturbation is one of the most common sources of sexual pleasure, so insulting someone by calling them a 'wanker' is foolish.) Both forms of mutual masturbation provide an enjoyable and safe way to come.

Kissing Lip to lip kissing is erotic for almost everyone and completely safe.

Body rubbing Moving your body up and down your partner's so that your genitals touch can be fun and carries no risks.

It's safe to come on each other's skin. (But not on cuts or sores.) 'Come on, not in!' is one of the safer sex mottos.

Stroking, body licking and massage

Running fingers up and down your partner's erogenous zones (back, chest, bum, thighs, feet, wherever gives them a thrill) is very pleasurable and entirely safe. Doing the same with your tongue, or massaging with your finger tips, is also erotic. When massaging, you might find that using baby oil or some other lotion will increase pleasure. All are safe and sensuous.

Nipple play Most men and women find their nipples to be sources of pleasure if squeezed, sucked and, if your partner is not too sensitive, gently bitten. There's no risk of HIV from these acts, but you may hurt your partner if you get carried away and bite too hard!

Sex aids Women can enjoy using vibrators which stimulate the clitoris, or dildos which are pushed into the vagina. Men sometimes like cock-rings which you push over the penis to help maintain an erection. These sex aids are safe but wash them after use.

SAFER SEX IS FUN

You will see that there are far more things you can do which are 'no risk' than 'low risk' or 'high risk'. So safer sex can mean a broader, more varied sex life, not a more limited one. Here are some more tips to ensure that safer sex is fun:

You don't have to 'screw' Many people enjoy sex which doesn't involve penetration but they do it because they think that that is what it means to have 'proper' sex. If you enjoy sex without this type of penetration, say so.

Condoms can be a turn-on A lot of people will want to enjoy penetration and worry that using condoms takes away the pleasure. ('Like doing it in a bin liner' as Danny says in Chapter

6). But using condoms can be erotic too: putting the condom on and applying the lubricant can be treated as part of the sexual build-up. You can get your partner to roll the condom on and rub on the lubricant while you rub it over and inside his or her genitals. If you are relaxed about it, it can be an erotic part of lovemaking and shows your partner you care.

Talking is the key One of the reasons that lots of people do have high risk, unsafe sex is that they feel too embarrassed to suggest alternatives. However, most people enjoy sex far more when they feel that they can discuss what pleases them and experiment with different activities. So take the plunge! Tell your partner – in a way that doesn't sound critical – exactly what you want to try. This kind of intimate love talk makes sex more fun and making a mutual decision to have safer sex will increase the sense of shared trust. If you can't communicate with your partner, should you be having sex anyway?

GETTING THE SAFER SEX YOU WANT

Knowing that you want safer sex is the first step towards protecting yourself. But sex researchers have found that people who know about AIDS and safer sex still sometimes end up having unsafe sex. The problem is often one of negotiation: How do you persuade your sexual partner that you want safer sex?

Here are some common objections to using condoms – and how to tackle them:

Slags carry condoms? It's sad that Kim believes that boys will think Rosa a slag if she pulls out a condom – but she could be right. Some men (and women) still have very old-fashioned and ridiculous ideas about women's sexuality. They think that it's the man's job to take all the initiative and that a woman who carries condoms must be shockingly 'forward'. This threatens their sense of masculinity.

If anyone accuses you of being a 'slag', don't be worried about showing your anger – you can tell them that if preventing the spread of a fatal illness means that you're a slag, it's better to be a slag than an idiot. If the person who says this is someone you're about to have sex with, you're probably better off not doing it at all with someone who's still got these attitudes.

Condoms kill pleasure? Some men will say things like: 'Using a condom's like having sex in a plastic bag', meaning that it reduces the sexual sensations. However, this is usually said by men who just can't be bothered. Condoms need not interfere with sexual pleasure and lots of couples who use them regularly don't find them any kind of problem. So if your partner objects to using them, suggest giving condoms another chance or doing something other than penetration.

It's a woman's job The kind of man who thinks that only 'slags' carry condoms is also the kind who often thinks that contraception is all up to the woman. So women can't expect men to carry condoms. If you can't change his attitude, bring your own condoms.

Are you saying I've got AIDS? Some people will think that insisting on safer sex is an insult, because you are implying that they have AIDS. They may think that you're suggesting they are gay or inject drugs, because they (wrongly) believe that only those people get AIDS. Explain that anyone can get AIDS and that it's thought that thousands of people have HIV without knowing it. Tell them, gently, that they should want to protect themselves and ignore the rubbish written in certain tabloid papers that states that only certain groups of people are at risk. Explain that you have no special reason for thinking that they have HIV, but you just don't want to risk it with anyone.

But I'm sure I'm okay Some people will try to convince you that there's no chance of getting the virus from them because they're sure that they haven't got it. In many cases this will be true but you have to ask yourself why someone who says there's no risk is happy to have unsafe sex with you. If you have any doubt, just say that you don't want to take the chance with anyone, and that you won't enjoy making love if you're worrying.

No condoms available If you are in the unlucky situation of wanting penetrative sex, but not being able to get any condoms, then insist on avoiding penetration and try some alternatives. Say that it gives you something to look forward to next time when you are prepared.

In general, most men and women don't want to risk AIDS or unwanted pregnancy and you should find that most partners will be relieved if you produce a condom.

DO YOU WANT A TEST?

If you are worried that you have HIV, you might want a test to find out. (There is no such thing as an AIDS test, only a test to find out if you have the virus which causes AIDS.) But before rushing to your nearest clinic, weigh up the pros and cons involved in this extremely important decision:

IN FAVOUR OF TESTING

■ If you don't have the virus, then it will set your mind at rest.

■ For some people, uncertainty is worse than bad news and knowing they have the virus might be better than constant worry.

■ You can change your lifestyle, begin to look after your health and protect your immune system. Cutting down smoking and drinking, and eating healthy food will help.

■ You may want to take anti-HIV drugs before you develop any symptoms of AIDS. Some doctors argue that this can delay the onset of illness, although there is no definite proof yet.

■ You may want to have a baby and need to know if there is a risk of passing the virus on.

AGAINST TESTING

■ Do you really want to know? If you do have HIV, this will probably make you extremely unhappy. Some people with AIDS think that the distress of discovering that they had the virus brought on the illness sooner than would have happened otherwise.

■ It is not certain that 100 per cent of people who have HIV will go on to develop AIDS. Even if they do, the average person will have the virus for several years before developing the syndrome. So provided you are practising safer sex, you might prefer to live in happy ignorance.

■ Unless you are certain that you and your partner don't have HIV, YOU SHOULD BE HAVING SAFER SEX AT ALL TIMES. If you are having safer sex, then it is not really important to have the test. You will not get the virus if you don't already have it and you won't pass it on if you do have it.

■ Some financial arrangements like getting mortgages and life insurance become more difficult if you have had a test.

■ Some people are so pleased to get a negative test result that they think they are risk free and stop practising safer sex.

HAVING A TEST

If you do decide to have an HIV test, here are some things to bear in mind:

■ Go to an STD (Sexually Transmitted Diseases) Clinic, rather than your doctor. The test is confidential but some people give a false name so that no pieces of paper with an HIV result connected to your name will ever be found.

■ You will have to have counselling before you have a test, so that you think through whether or not you really want it. You will be sent away to think through your decision and asked to come back if you still want a test. You should also get counselling after the test, if it proves positive.

■ If you have the test on the National Health Service, you will have to wait two weeks before getting the result.

■ If you are tested and don't have the virus, don't think that this means you're invulnerable. Carry on having safer sex.

■ If you have got HIV, then there are various groups and organizations which you can turn to for help. ◮

TO FIND OUT MORE

For excellent free booklets on AIDS and Safer Sex contact The Terrence Higgins Trust. ◮

Make It Happy, Make It Safe, Jane Cousins-Mills, published by Penguin.

♥ ♥ ♥ ♥ ♥

BIRTH CONTROL

SO THERE YOU GO! MY OLD MAN'S IDEA WASN'T SO BAD.

BIT LATE THOUGH. I ALREADY KNEW IT ALL.

YEAH! ADULTS DON'T REALIZE WHAT KIDS GET UP TO AT TWELVE!

EXACTLY!

OH! SO WHAT WERE YOU UP TO?

ER...I CAN'T REMEMBER. I ONLY...I....

HA HA!

WHY ARE YOU BLUSHING DANNY?

I'M NOT!

LOVE + LUST

HOT HOT

chapter six

BIRTH CONTROL

A lot of people like Danny think they know all about birth control. But when it comes to it, they're not too sure and because they don't want to look foolish, they don't like to ask.

Here are some facts about different methods of birth control so that you can choose the method that's right for you and your partner. Just as it takes two people to make a baby, so preventing pregnancy is a joint responsibility.

It only takes one sperm to fertilize the egg and each time you have sex which includes penetration and ejaculation, millions of sperm are released. So unless the sperm are prevented from going up the vagina and meeting the egg in the womb, pregnancy is very likely to happen. However, birth control is widely available these days (unless you live in Northern Ireland) so there's no reason for any woman to get pregnant unless she chooses to.

There are still a lot of myths around about how not to get pregnant. Here are some of them: they are ALL FALSE.

YOU CAN'T GET PREGNANT IF

■ you do it standing up.
■ you go to the loo or have a bath straight afterwards.
■ it's the first time.
■ the girl doesn't have an orgasm.
■ you make love during your period.
■ he doesn't put it all the way in.
■ he comes out straight afterwards.

OH YES YOU CAN!

You can also get pregnant through interrupted intercourse ('coitus interruptus') which used to be popular among young people. It's when the boy promises to pull out just before he comes. Apart from making things tense for both partners, this is very unreliable since some drops of semen (the fluid which contains millions of sperm) often escape from the penis before ejaculation. It's so much more fun and safer to use a condom!

So what are the ways of making sure that you control your reproductive system rather than your body controlling you?

SAYING NO

This isn't a joke! If you are really worried that you could become pregnant and either you don't want to use birth control or you haven't anything with you, then this anxiety will spoil your enjoyment of sex. Why not agree not to have penetrative sex until you are fully prepared? There are lots of ways to have fun and play around together without having penetration. (See Chapter 5.) Never feel pushed into having sex until you are sure it's right for you.

CONDOMS

(johnny, rubber, sheath, Durex, Mates) These are the only contraceptives which will protect you from catching the HIV virus that causes AIDS as well as stopping you getting pregnant. Condoms are about 95 per cent effective against pregnancy.

Condoms should be used with a spermicide cream called nonoxynol, which kills both the sperm and the HIV virus. If you have any doubts about your partner's sexual history (and who can be really sure?) or your own, then this method is essential. (See Chapter 5.)

Here's how to use one – it may seem fiddly at first but practice makes perfect:

■ Always choose a brand that carries the British Safety Standards kite mark. Take it carefully out of its packet. DO NOT unroll it.

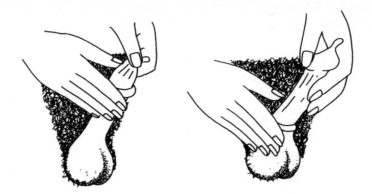

■ Pinch the little teat at the end of the condom to keep the air out. This leaves a space for the semen or come to collect.

■ Hold the condom over the tip of the erect penis and carefully roll it down the sides until the whole penis is covered in the thin rubber.

■ Although some condoms already have spermicide cream on them, it's a good idea to smear extra cream from a tube onto the penis or in the vagina or anus before intercourse.

■ After ejaculation (coming), the boy should withdraw his penis while holding onto the bottom of the condom so it comes out still covering the penis. This makes sure no drops of semen leak out.

■ Take it off and tie a knot in it to stop the semen spilling out. Wrap it in tissues and throw away. It's unwise to flush condoms down the loo because they can block the drains.

■ Use a new condom each time you make love. Once you get the hang of using condoms, it takes just seconds. Your partner can help put it on and it can even be a turn-on! You can buy them from chemists, supermarkets or machines, or get them free from Family

Planning Clinics. Girls can carry condoms as well as boys and it's a good way of sharing responsibility for birth control.

THE PILL

The Pill revolutionized birth control in the sixties by giving women a simple and effective way of controlling their fertility. It was partly responsible for the so-called Free Love movement of that time and some women felt it put pressure on them to be sexually available.

There were also worries that not enough research had been done on the long-term effects of the chemicals in the Pill, and some women still object to the idea of taking 'unnatural' chemicals into their bodies. Some people have also objected to the way early trials of the Pill were carried out on poor, Third World women. The Pill's great advantage is that it is taken at a regular time each day and it isn't directly connected with the act of lovemaking. It's about 98 per cent effective against pregnancy and also gives you a regular monthly cycle. The so-called mini-Pill is now very popular and contains lower levels of chemicals.

The Pill works by releasing artificial hormones which prevent the woman's egg from ripening. Since the egg isn't released from the ovary, there's no chance of conception, so you can't get pregnant. Once you stop taking the Pill, you start producing eggs again.

There are now many different types of Pill available and it's a matter of talking to your doctor about which is best for you. Some have side effects like feeling sick or gaining weight but most women find one which their body gets used to. It is a bad idea to take the Pill if you smoke more than a couple of cigarettes a day because the combination could increase your risk of heart disease.

IUD (Coil, Loop)

IUD stands for 'intrauterine device', which means something put inside the uterus or womb to stop pregnancy taking place. It's about 95 per cent effective. The IUD is a small metal or plastic object which has to be inserted by a specially trained doctor or health worker. It is put into the womb through the small hole in the cervix. This takes just a few seconds but it can be painful, like a sharp period cramp. The cramps may continue for a day or two but once your body gets used to the IUD, you can't feel it's there. You may find you bleed more heavily during your period.

The IUD can be pushed out so it's important to check once a week that it's still in place. It has a couple of threads attached which go through the cervix and can be felt inside the vagina so that you can make sure it is in place. If you can't feel the threads, go straight back to your doctor.

Like the Pill, the IUD is a convenient form of birth control and is almost as safe as the Pill without the side effects. However, it can lead to infections and some women can't get along with it. Some doctors believe it is less suitable for girls who haven't had a baby.

DIAPHRAGM (Cap)

This is one of the simplest methods once you've got the hang of inserting it. It's known as a barrier method, like using a condom, because the diaphragm forms a barrier which prevents the sperm entering the womb. It must always be used with a spermicide like nonoxynol, and if used properly it's almost as effective as the Pill.

The diaphragm is a flexible wire ring covered in thin rubber, a bit like a small Frisbee. Diaphragms come in different sizes and the doctor or nurse at the clinic will choose the right size for you. They'll show you how to cover it in spermicidal cream or jelly and then push it up inside your vagina so that it fits snugly over your cervix. When it's in place, you and your partner can't feel it.

You can put it in no more than three hours before you make love. You leave it in for eight hours to make sure all the sperm are killed. If you have sex more than once, you should put some more cream inside the vagina using an applicator.

It's easy to remove the diaphragm by hooking your finger under it and pulling. It can't possibly get stuck inside you or disappear. Then wash and dry it carefully and put it back in its plastic case. Check it regularly to make sure the rubber hasn't perished and there are no small holes.

You should get a new diaphragm fitted each year in case you need a different size. Don't ever lend your diaphragm to a friend - it probably won't be the right size for her. And remember, the diaphragm will only work if it's inside you - not in your handbag!

EMERGENCY MEASURES

If you have had sex without using any contraceptive (known as 'unprotected intercourse'), there are a couple of things you can do to prevent pregnancy. One is to have an IUD inserted as soon as possible within the next few days. Or you can take emergency contraceptive pills.

Sometimes known as 'the morning-after Pill', it should be called the three-day-after Pill because it is effective in preventing conception if taken within three days of the unprotected intercourse. Your doctor or Family Planning Clinic can prescribe them. They are like taking a very large dose of birth control pills and can make you feel quite ill during the day that you take them. They are for emergencies only.

NEW DEVELOPMENTS

Despite all these choices, birth control is still far from perfect. There are a few new devices which are being tested at the moment and could be available within the next year or so:

The female condom A thin rubber tube which fits inside the vagina, covering all the vaginal wall. It is an alternative to using a condom and will protect against HIV as well as pregnancy.

Vaginal ring A flexible ring which is placed inside the vagina and can be left there for three months. It contains hormones which are slowly released into the body and work like the Pill to prevent pregnancy.

Hormonal implant A small implant inserted under the skin which also slowly releases hormones to prevent conception. It will work for three months before it needs to be replaced.

Hormonal patch A small sticky plaster patch which goes on your bottom or upper thigh. It operates like the implant but has to be changed each week.

WHO AM I?

chapter seven

WHO AM I?

Most people want to feel 'normal', especially about something as sensitive as love and sex. It's easy to laugh at people who seem weird or abnormal - unless you're the one being laughed at. Then it's about as funny as a boot in the face. And there are particularly strong pressures to conform when it comes to sexual identity.

Most people will grow up to be heterosexual, but this doesn't mean that they are attracted solely to the opposite sex throughout their lives. Many people will find themselves attracted to their own sex as well as the opposite sex at some time, and young people in particular may feel confused and afraid as a result.

In fact, what's normal for one person may feel quite strange to another. For instance, someone who has not made love for the last ten years might find the idea of sex really peculiar. It's important to discover what's normal for you and to be able to ignore insults from ignorant people who are frightened of others who aren't just like them.

SEXUAL IDENTITY: THESE ARE THE TERMS

Human sexual feelings and behaviour are a lot less cut and dried than most of the world wants to admit. Researchers at the Kinsey Institute in America devised a five-point scale of sexual identity ranging from total heterosexuality to total homosexuality. It was found that very few people were 100 per cent gay or straight. Most people's sexuality fell somewhere in between. In other words, the potential for homo- or bi-sexuality exists in most of us.

So labels such as 'gay' and 'straight' are basically artificial, like most attempts to make people fit into categories. Trying to apply them to yourself may make you feel even more confused than before, particularly if your feelings and fancies don't fit into any particular slot. But helpful or unhelpful, almost everybody uses these terms. So what do they mean?

Heterosexual or 'straight' Someone who is 100 per cent heterosexual will be exclusively attracted to the opposite sex. ('Hetero' means 'other' in Greek.) Many people who identify themselves as straight may at some time have been attracted to their own sex, but are mainly straight. One recent survey estimated that at least 30 per cent of heterosexual men have had a homosexual experience at some time in their lives.

Homosexual - gay and lesbian Someone who is only attracted to the same sex ('homo' meaning 'same' in Greek) is described as homosexual. Both men and women can be called 'homosexual' but men tend to prefer 'gay' and women the word 'lesbian', as these labels sound less clinical. It's estimated that about 10 per cent of adults are homosexual.

Bisexual People who are sexually attracted to both sexes are what's known as 'bisexual'. ('Bi' is Greek for two.) Since sex researchers believe that most people have the capacity to be bisexual, it's more practical to think of someone as bisexual only if they are strongly attracted to and have made love to both sexes.

HOW DO YOU KNOW WHAT YOU ARE?

These labels aren't always so easy to apply when it comes to identifying your own sexuality. For instance, if you are mainly attracted to members of the opposite sex, but very strongly attracted to one member of your own sex, are you straight, gay or bisexual? There is no right answer. These labels don't describe the way a lot of people feel or take into account the complexities of love and desire.

They also imply that someone's sexuality is fixed for all time. But in fact, people's sexuality can change and develop throughout their life.

It is very common in your teens to feel strong attraction ('crushes') towards members of your own sex – a teacher or older student, for instance. These intense romantic and sexual feelings may lead you to think that you are gay, only to find that when you start becoming sexually active, your desires are completely heterosexual. On the other hand, you may assume that you are straight and then suddenly, aged twenty-five or fifty-five, find yourself swept off your feet by a member of your own fair sex.

Of course, you may have no problems working out your sexuality. You may only be attracted to the opposite sex and never question this or you may know you are gay from a very young age. However, if you don't feel 100 per cent gay or straight, you certainly should not see yourself as some freakish sexual misfit. Keep these points in mind:

■ These labels are artificial and it's their problem not yours if none of them fit.

■ If you keep changing your mind about your sexual identity, relax and try to forget about defining yourself for a while.

■ What's really important is loving an individual and having a satisfying relationship with them, whatever their sex.

■ If you think you may be lesbian or gay, you are not alone. It's estimated that about 10 per cent of the population is with you. All you have to do is find them! The lesbian and gay organizations can help you to do this. ▣

■ Don't worry if everyone around you seems to be sorted out except for you. The chances are they're feeling much the same but are too afraid to show it.

GLAD TO BE GAY?

Many young people who realize that they are lesbian or gay feel far from glad about it. Although they'll usually become more optimistic later on, at first they may feel despairing and believe their lives are ruined. So it's worth bearing these positive points in mind:

Girls like girls and boys like boys In this society, boys and girls are often brought up not to understand one another: to play different games, have different aims and socialize separately. This means that heterosexual couples often have difficulty understanding each other's feelings. Lesbians and gay men draw their partners from the sex they've been brought up to get on with. This helps to avoid problems arising from the 'battle of the sexes' which heterosexuals undergo.

Understanding how the body works As well as emotional differences, there are physical differences and straights often complain that their partners don't know how to make love with them properly. 'She holds it all wrong' or 'he rubs far too hard' are common complaints. Because you know how your own body works, you may understand more about your partner's sexuality. So although we are all different with individual desires, lesbians and gays may have a head start when it comes to sexual satisfaction.

No fear of pregnancy Birth control methods are still far from perfect and since homosexual couples can't get pregnant, this is one problem you avoid. Of course, it's crucial to practise safer sex. (See Chapter 5.)

No children As homosexual couples cannot biologically have children, many people see this as a major drawback and sacrifice. (Some lesbians do become pregnant with the help of a friendly male or Artificial Insemination and bring up the baby with their girlfriends.) But many gay relationships flourish without the pressures of childrearing and many homosexual couples live happily together for many years just as heterosexual couples do. Children are sometimes the reason why loveless and unhappy marriages survive, causing pain to children and parents. Without children, you have greater freedom of choice over your relationships and need only stay together because you really love and care for each other.

Standing up for your sexuality Although 'coming out' can be a painful and difficult experience, it can also be a liberating one. The courage and self-awareness required to come out may make you a stronger and more aware person. From feeling ashamed of yourself and your sexuality, you can go on to take more pride in your identity than many heterosexuals who have never had to face that challenge.

Creative outsiders Traditionally, being homosexual has isolated people from the mainstream of society. But that position as an outsider has produced some very creative and perceptive commentators on life. There is a large number of great artists and thinkers who have been bisexual or preferred to love their own sex: Sappho, Plato, Michelangelo, Oscar Wilde, Tennessee Williams, Virginia Woolf, David Hockney, James Baldwin and Martina Navratilova are just a few.

In the end, what is important in any relationship is the quality of that relationship, not the gender of the partners. The right person for you is the person you love and enjoy making love with, regardless of gender.

PREJUDICE AND 'COMING OUT'

If 10 per cent of the population is estimated to be gay, many more worry that they might be homosexual at some time in their lives. This fear of their potential for homosexuality may partly explain the strong anti-gay feelings many straights have. (This is known as 'homophobia'.) Many straight men are also very threatened by lesbians who don't need to depend on men for sex or love.

These feelings are backed up by the clichéd images of homosexuals in the media, particularly in the kind of television sit-com Danny and Co were watching. Gay men are not automatically limp-wristed, effeminate and high-voiced, nor are lesbians automatically fat and butch in dungarees. It just suits certain people to think that, so they can dismiss what threatens them as being as ridiculous and weird. Rosa and Max are right when they brand the old-fashioned stereotypes as pathetic. They aren't even especially funny either.

Whatever the reasons, lesbians and gays still have to put up with a lot of hassle in this country. For example:

■ Sex between consenting men in private is only legal at twenty-one, five years older than for straights. The law doesn't recognize the existence of lesbianism so the age limit for lesbians is the same as for heterosexuals, i.e. sixteen years.

■ Laws of public order and decency can be used against homosexuals kissing or openly showing affection to each other.

■ Gay couples cannot marry in the UK. (In Denmark they can have a civil marriage with the economic advantages that go with it.)

■ Lesbian and gay individuals and couples cannot adopt children. At present some local authorities allow gay couples to foster children but this is under review.

■ Gay people may be discriminated against at work or when seeking a job. This is a reason why many gays choose to stay 'in the closet'.

■ People who are suspected of being gay are sometimes abused, beaten up and even killed in incidents known as 'gay bashing'.

WHAT TO DO?

If you are worried about any of the issues mentioned in this chapter, it's essential to talk them over with a sympathetic person. You may feel lonely and isolated but do make an effort to get support and talk to someone about your feelings. These are the options:

■ Tell a friend. Most good friends will give you a better reaction than you expect and may even turn out to have similar feelings. But sexuality is a touchy issue and there is a small chance that your friend may give you a hostile reaction. That's your friend's problem, not yours.

■ Think about telling your parents. It can be very difficult and upsetting hiding important aspects of yourself from your family. If your parents react sympathetically, this will ease your mind and improve your relationship with them. However, some parents react very badly because of their ignorance and anxiety.

If you think your parents may react negatively, it might be better to wait until you are more independent. Many parents will find the news a shock at first but will come to accept and respect your sexuality in time.

■ Contact a lesbian, gay or bisexual organization. This is the most reliable way to get support and advice. You should phone your local Lesbian and Gay Switchboard number, where you will speak to trained counsellors. △ They will talk to you about your feelings and recommend organizations and groups that you can contact. There is also a network of local groups for bisexuals. △

TO FIND OUT MORE

Out in Europe, Peter Tatchell, published by Channel 4 (available from PO Box 4000, London W3 6XJ).
How to be a Happy Homosexual: A Guide For Gay Men, Terry Sanderson, published by Gay Men's Press.
Being Lesbian, Lorraine Trenchard, published by Gay Men's Press.

COPING WITH LOVE

74

chapter eight

COPING WITH LOVE

Making love isn't just about bodies. It's about hearts and minds too. Sometimes it's easy to forget that sex is an emotional as well as physical experience – until you fall in love, that is. Falling in love when you are young can feel very intense precisely because you are new to affairs of the heart. It's often hard to predict how you're going to feel about someone you're getting to know and strong feelings can develop very quickly.

Love, as we're told every day in pop songs and on television, can be the most brilliant feeling in the world. I happen to be writing this on Valentine's Day and everywhere the joys of love are being exploited to make us spend money on cards, flowers and gifts. Partly because of all this hype, a lot of people can't wait to throw themselves into a love affair as soon as possible. But relationships can be messy and painful as well as enjoyable, so it's worth knowing about the tears as well as the hearts and flowers.

Unless you're very lucky, or just easily pleased, you probably won't find somebody who is right for you for when you first start looking for a partner. It takes time to begin to know yourself and to form an idea of the kind of person who suits you. And just as important, it takes time to choose the kind of relationship you want.

Most of us are taught to think that relationships follow a simple pattern: you meet, fall in love, get together and then just get on with it. Reality is a lot more complicated and you need to make some tough decisions. There are lots of ways to have a relationship and these choices apply whether you are gay or straight.

Monogamy This means an exclusive commitment to a one-to-one relationship, in which neither you nor your partner has sex with anyone else. Most people assume that their relationship should and will be monogamous. For many people this works and they could not imagine being happy any other way. However, others say they will be monogamous and then change their minds. This can make their lover feel betrayed and unhappy and may lead to the end of the relationship.

Serial monogamy This means that you are monogamous but you do not expect one relationship to last forever. So you are likely to have a series of monogamous relationships. This is probably more realistic than the traditional 'happy ever after' expectations although a lot of people do have one relationship which lasts a lifetime.

Open relationships Also known as polygamy, these relationships involve an agreement between the partners that they can have sex outside the central relationship. It's argued that since no one person can fulfil all another's needs, this is the most 'natural' and satisfying set-up. It can also be more honest since there is no pretence at being faithful. However, in open relationships one partner is often much keener on polygamy than the other! The other may just go along with it while feeling jealous and unhappy inside. These kinds of relationships can involve risks because no one can ever be sure that a 'casual sexual partner' will remain casual. Sex involves intimacy which can lead to love.

Sleeping with friends Some people like to have a group of friends with whom they sometimes have sex. As long as there isn't any jealousy between the friends, and everyone practises safer sex, this can turn out to be fun and supportive for all. However, if you fall seriously in love with someone, either inside or outside the group, you may find yourself thinking these sexual relationships were quite shallow in comparison. And introducing sex into a friendship may change or spoil the friendship.

Sex with no strings Intense sexual relationships with no strings attached is what some people prefer. They may be highly sexual or threatened by emotion and commitment and just don't want to mix sex with love. They may get their intimacy and emotional support from friends rather than lovers, because lovers make too many demands on their freedom. If this is what you want, try to be honest with your partners from the beginning. And bear in mind that no one is immune from falling in love! Above all, if you want to go for casual sex, make it safe. The more partners, the higher the risk of catching a sexually transmitted disease.

LOVE HURTS: PROBLEMS WITH RELATIONSHIPS

As you can see, there are lots of different ways to have fulfilling relationships. Unfortunately, there are also lots of ways that love can lead to problems:

Obsession It's not uncommon to develop an obsession about someone you're having a relationship with or would like to get to know. The obsessional signs include thinking about him or her all the time; feeling physically ill with anxiety or excitement; being unable to work, sleep or eat; believing you could never be happy without that person and could never love anyone else.

Of course, some of these feelings are a normal part of falling in love, but if they become an obsession they can be damaging to you and will almost certainly scare off the object of your desires. This kind of love is more about your own fantasy trip than loving the other person. If you are unhappy, it's all to easy to think that the other person can be the solution to all your problems. Sadly, this is never the case. If obsessions like this carry on, you should think about getting some counselling. ◲

Jealousy Some people hardly seem to suffer from jealousy at all, but lots of people are very jealous indeed. They are constantly afraid of their partner leaving them for someone else and they may hate them to see or mention ex-lovers. They may be suspicious if their partner is in the company of anyone whom they think fancies them and may even become jealous of friends or family.

If you suffer from the 'green-eyed monster' try to fight it. You'll make yourself very unhappy agonizing over your partner's feelings and behaviour. No one can possess another person and you'll only upset them with your suspicious behaviour. You'll also make them feel you don't trust them and this can kill a relationship stone dead.

Jealousy is usually based on your own insecurity and lack of self-esteem – so try to work on improving that. If there is some reason to be jealous, it's far better to discuss what's going on and what you and partner want in a rational way rather than exploding with jealous anger. Again, counselling can help this obsession. ◲

Losing friends Some relationships become so absorbing and time-consuming that you stop seeing your old friends. Sometimes your partner won't want you to see them because they want you all to themselves. Often boys simply expect girls to give up their friends and to fit themselves around his mates. But however in love you feel, try to resist giving up your previous life completely. After all, your lover fell for you because of who you were so don't change too much.

It is important, even if you do have less time for your friends, not to let yourself become isolated with only your partner for company. If you do, you will feel much more dependent on your lover and this may put a strain on the relationship. Once the first thrills of love have worn off, you may find yourself missing your friends and feeling lonely. Love should widen your horizons, not narrow them!

Changing people It's a common myth that falling in love will change someone and make them into a 'better' person. Of course we all thrive on love and giving and receiving love can certainly make us more secure and happier. But if you fall for someone with a lot of problems, don't fool yourself into thinking that you are going to change them overnight. This is a common trap and can have disastrous consequences.

If you fall in love with an alcoholic or a drug addict, even though they may promise to change and kick the habit, their problem may be bigger than both of you. So think hard before you take it on. The best way of loving an addict is to give them the support to get expert help to tackle the problem for themselves. (See Chapter 11 on getting off drugs.)

Power and abuse Love thrives on taking turns and sharing - in other words, on equality. The best relationships exist when both people have roughly equal amounts of control. If you find that you're getting into a relationship in which either you are dominated or you completely dominate your partner, then you know something's wrong. For example, if you make all the decisions, then you will probably soon get bored. You'd do better to look for partners with stronger opinions and more confidence in themselves. If your partner makes all the decisions and gets their own way all the time, you're liable to end up feeling powerless and resentful.

In the most extreme cases of inequality of power, women will become trapped in relationships with men who abuse them. This abuse may consist of either psychological torment or actual physical abuse. Women in these situations can grow to hate themselves and feel that they deserve to be punished. If you ever find yourself in this mess, get counselling and support to escape. There are several organizations and refuges to turn to. It is your life and your body and no one has the right to abuse you. ◭

BREAKING UP

The obvious solution to relationships with severe problems is to end them. But this is more easily said than done. Although breaking up shouldn't be too difficult for most young people who don't have a marriage, mortgage or children to hold them together, many people find that breaking up is hard to do. Here are some typical situations and ways of dealing with them:

Dependent partner You may want to finish a relationship but are afraid to because your partner says they can't live without you. So you hang on. This kind of situation can often continue even when the dependent person is abusing you. It's common for a man who regularly beats his partner to keep on saying sorry afterwards and pleading with her to stay. Remaining with a partner because you feel guilty about leaving is a very bad reason for staying. You can't stay because of guilt forever and the longer you leave it, the harder it gets.

If you really can't face the other person's distress or attempts to change your mind, then suggest a trial separation or even write a letter putting your reasons for finishing on paper. This shows you are serious and really want to change the situation. Even if your partner swears they can't live without you, they will probably find someone else fairly soon. Dependent personalities need someone to cling to and they are often not that choosy about who it is.

Promises of change As we said earlier, people don't change very easily and if you're only staying with someone because they are promising to change, then set a time limit. For instance, if your partner is an alcoholic, you'd be best advised to recommend they go to Alcoholics Anonymous and resume the relationship if and when they've kicked the habit.

N o t h i n g   b e t t e r You may be fed up with your relationship but scared to leave it because there is no immediate replacement partner on the horizon. This is a very bad reason to continue. There is nothing wrong with being on your own for a while. In fact, it's usually a lot better than being in a relationship that isn't working. So take the plunge and use your new free time to do all the things you've been meaning to do for ages.

T h e   g r a s s   i s   g r e e n e r Relationships, even very good, loving ones, often reach a point when you no longer feel in love. You take your partner for granted and even though you know that you love them, it doesn't excite you to be with them any longer. So you may consider finishing it or even start a flirtation with someone new. Think hard! You may be throwing away a good relationship for something which will only provide a few weeks of excitement.

No relationship remains at the same intensity forever and they go through good and bad phases. You have to work at relationships to keep them fresh and exciting, so look at what you can do to revive your feelings for each other before you head for 'new pastures'.

COPING WITH REJECTION

If you're the one who is dumped and the relationship falls apart despite all your efforts, you will naturally feel very upset. Give yourself time to feel this loss and to talk about those feelings to friends. Don't just bottle up your emotions to appear tough, and try to keep a positive attitude about the future. Here are a few tips:

■ DON'T feel that you'll never trust anyone ever again. It's horrible to feel rejected and betrayed but just because it's happened once, doesn't mean it will happen again.

■ DON'T brood over your ex-partner or allow yourself to think that you'll never love anyone else. Once you've got through the pain, you might find yourself falling for someone else quite soon, even if that seems impossible at the moment.

■ DON'T ring your ex-partner up at 3 a.m., or keep hovering around their doorstep, begging to be taken back. This kind of behaviour only makes you look and feel pathetic and puts the other person off even more. You'll feel much better and recover quicker if you try to behave in a dignified way.

■ DON'T stop looking after yourself by letting your appearance go and getting drunk all the time. This kind of masochism may seem romantic in the movies but it won't help. You might feel less attractive for a while after being rejected but this is the time to start picking yourself up. Look to the future and make the most of yourself.

These tips look fine on paper but are difficult to put into practice. It's all too easy to tell someone to pull themselves together when they feel that they're falling apart. However, many young people, particularly girls, waste a lot of time in their teens getting upset over relationships which later they realize weren't that important. If you're that kind of person, try to develop more confidence and convince yourself that you don't need someone who doesn't need you.

LONELY HEARTS

As we said, some people put up with unhappy relationships because they are frightened to be alone. They feel they only exist as part of a couple. There is a lot of pressure from society to 'bond' as soon as possible. Try to resist this. Being single can be great fun and very productive. You may learn more about yourself and about life by keeping your independence and operating from your own base. So try not to feel you have to be in a relationship just for the sake of it.

But there are many people who feel they have spent long enough alone and would love to meet someone. Here are some reasons why you may be finding it difficult to get a relationship off the ground - and some ways of tackling the problem.

Too young? Some young people feel pressurized into 'going out' with someone just because their friends are doing it. They aren't really ready for a relationship and as a result remain single for longer than some of their friends. There is nothing wrong with this so just relax and wait until you feel ready or get swept off your feet!

Too unattractive? You may be totally lacking in self-confidence and feel you're too unattractive for anyone to fancy. In fact, being conventionally good-looking doesn't have much to do with sexual attraction. With a more positive attitude, you might be surprised by how many people do fancy you.

If you want to improve your appearance, get together with a good friend and discuss changes you could make. A different hair style or just more frequent hair washing? A new look? But bear in mind that personality and attitude are just as important as appearance. (See Chapter 9 on body image.)

Too insecure about your sexuality? If you're a young lesbian or gay man, you may find it very difficult to meet other people who will openly tell you that they are homosexual too. Or you may not have sorted out whether you are gay or not. Most people in this situation feel really lonely and isolated until they find someone to talk to. Luckily, there are excellent organizations set up just to meet this need so don't be afraid to contact them. Your local Lesbian and Gay Switchboard will put you in touch with your nearest lesbian and gay group or you can get some counselling over the telephone. (See Chapter 6 on sexual identity.) ◪

Too choosy? You might have plenty of people keen on you but you just aren't interested in them because they don't measure up to your ideal partner. If you're happy that way, then fine. However, if you feel disappointed, you should start looking more closely at the people around you. You may find them more interesting and attractive than you thought at first. Your high expectations may be a way of protecting yourself from contact with others by playing it cool or hankering after an unrealistic image of the perfect boy or girlfriend.

Too frightened of being hurt? Although you may think you want a relationship, you may be frightened of taking the plunge, especially if you've seen friends get their fingers burnt. Getting involved with other people is always a risky business and love can hurt. But most of us think the pleasure outweighs the pain!

chapter nine

MORE
BODY TALK

The pressures to be physically 'perfect' are greater in this society than ever before - perhaps because there's so much money in it. As Robert noticed, advertisements bombard us with images of what we are supposed to look like. Since very few people do fit the fashion model stereotype, most of us end up feeling inadequate and unattractive.

These feelings are often strongest in our teens. At that time, we don't have a very clear body image, and our bodies are changing in ways that we may not immediately enjoy. We can be seduced by the media images and forget that people who look nothing like models can be extremely attractive.

As a result, a lot of people end up hating their bodies and feeling miserable. It's not just women who suffer. There is increasing pressure on men to look right - tall, muscular and slim, wearing the latest fashion. And those who don't shape up can feel pretty bad. Even 'right-on' Robert worries about his hair!

However, what a woman looks like is still much more important in this society than how a man looks. So it is women who suffer the greatest feelings of anxiety about their appearance. Young women who don't fit the norm - they may be 'overweight', have very small breasts or be 'too tall' - are often made to feel as if they are misfits with no sexuality of their own.

This kind of treatment is not just unkind, it's ridiculous and even dangerous. Increasing numbers of young people in America are going to cosmetic surgeons to change their looks with surgery. This is an unnecessary, risky and expensive step to take and a sure sign of a society obsessed with body image.

What makes someone attractive is a complex mixture of factors which combine to give them their individuality. It's the way someone's body blends with their voice, body language and gestures and above all, their attitude and personality. The best way to look good is to feel good about yourself - but it's easier said than done.

LOVE YOUR BODY

To help you feel better about your body, think about these points:

■ There is no such thing as one standard of physical beauty. Fashions and tastes change every year (that's how they get us to spend money on a new look) and people can be attractive in completely different ways. Look at some old paintings to see how the standards of female beauty have changed throughout the ages. Botticelli's plump and luscious Venus certainly wouldn't fit into a size ten.

■ Luckily, we all have very different tastes and preferences and these change throughout our lives. One friend of mine only fancies tall, blond, skinny men. Another always falls for short, Jewish Americans, preferably bald!

■ Having confidence in yourself is more likely to make you appear attractive to others. This doesn't mean you have to strut around or follow the latest fashions. Choose clothes you feel good in, make sure you look and smell clean and fresh and then forget about it. There's no greater turn-off than someone constantly looking in the mirror or checking themselves out all the time.

■ If you learn to like your own body – however unlike the current image of beauty it might be – you are likely to find that other people also find you attractive. Try to overcome your self-consciousness and relax.

If you are in a sexual relationship, it's worth getting used to walking around naked and not feeling shy in front of your partner. What's the point of undressing in the dark or getting into bed fully clothed? It's more likely to draw attention to the fat belly you are trying to hide. For years, I walked around with my head tilted back trying to hide a double chin until I realized that no one except me noticed the tiny fold of flesh. They just thought I was stuck up!

■ Your mood and personality really do show on your face and in your body language. A grumpy or sulky look could put people off however much time or money you've spent on your outfit. Someone with a smile and a lively interest in life is more likely to be welcome.

■ Think about the people you know and fancy. Do they conform to the mainstream standard of good looks? I doubt it. So if you can fancy them, other people can fancy you even if you aren't typical model material.

TOO FAT TO LOVE?

One of the most common body image obsessions centres around weight and shape. Women are most likely to be the victims. Most women in our society are made to feel that they are fat partly because models and female film-stars are far thinner than most of us who are healthy eaters. In fact, 70 per cent of women are on a diet at any one time – a terrible statistic and a terrible waste of time and money, except for the people who sell diet books and diet foods.

Dieting can damage your health and encourage the obsession with how you look. Most people who do lose weight by dieting put it on again within a few months. But it isn't surprising that women are always trying to get thinner because bigger women are looked down on in this society and calling someone 'fat' is a term of abuse. The subtle message is that men prefer women to look 'petite and feminine' i.e. weak and powerless. Large women are made to feel they are not sexual people because they don't fit the sex-symbol stereotype.

Provided you have a healthy diet with not too much sugar and fat, the best solution is to learn to enjoy your body as it is. After all, the idea that 'thin is beautiful' is a fairly recent idea – a hundred years ago men and women who are now considered fat would have been thought beautiful. (There are parts of the world now where fat women have higher status and are proud of their size.) It's more important to be healthy and fit than slim, so take lots of exercise, eat sensibly and stop jumping on the scales.

EATING DISORDERS

Unfortunately, some people get so obsessed by the idea that they have to get thin that it takes over their life. Here are some eating disorders which seem to be on the increase among young people:

A n o r e x i a   n e r v o s a Someone who is obsessed with their body size and with losing weight and who will go to great lengths to starve themselves has an illness called anorexia. Many women who have anorexia talk about it as an extreme form of control over their bodies. They get satisfaction out of setting themselves rigid goals and losing enough weight to reach them. This eventually takes over their life and although anorexics eat very little, they are constantly hungry and obsessed with food.

Anorexics have a very distorted view of their body image and often see themselves as fat even though they are painfully thin. They usually have deep-rooted psychological problems, often connected with their family. They may also have a fear of becoming sexually mature. One of the effects of self-starvation is that your periods stop and you lose sexual desire.

Anorexia is a very complex illness, and without proper treatment, the sufferer can starve herself to death. (Boys can suffer from this illness too - about 10 per cent of anorexics are male.) Therapy and other specialist help is usually needed to overcome the problem. Anyone who thinks that they might be anorexic should contact the Eating Disorders Association, as soon as possible. If you think a friend may have the problem, encourage them to get help, although they may be reluctant to admit there's anything wrong. ▲

Eating Disorders Association has local groups around the country. Your doctor may provide help, but some GPs, particularly male doctors, may not be very sympathetic. Change your doctor and get help as quickly as possible. ▲

B u l i m i a   Someone who binges (for example, eating the whole contents of the fridge in the middle of the night) and then gets rid of the food by making themselves vomit or taking laxatives is bulimic. A lot of anorexics are bulimic too. As well as indicating severe psychological problems, this can cause long-term damage to the sufferer's teeth, throat and stomach because of all the acid in their vomit. Follow the same steps as advised for anorexia nervosa and seek expert help. ▲

C o m p u l s i v e   e x e r c i s e   This is becoming more common with the current fitness obsessions. If you find that doing and thinking about exercise is taking over your life, work out a sensible timetable and stick to it. No one needs to jog or do aerobics for hours each day. Compulsive exercise can also be a form of anorexia and expert help may be needed.

PHYSICAL DISABILITY

People with physical disabilities are probably the group most badly affected by our society's standards of physical 'perfection'. This can make it very hard for them to form loving and sexual relationships.

Many able-bodied people find it hard to come to terms with their own sexuality and the thought of a disabled member of the family or friend having a sex life is just too much for them to contemplate. As a result, people with disabilities are often deprived of one of life's pleasures.

The more people differ from what is put forward as the physical 'norm', the less families, friends and doctors expect or allow them to express their sexuality. They may even be stopped from masturbating, particularly if they live in an institution and don't have their privacy. Their friends and carers may assume that because their bodies may not be conventionally 'pleasing' to look at, they don't have sexual desires and are not sexually attractive to others. As a result they are treated like children and patronized.

People with disabilities have sexual desires like anyone else and have a right to their own sex life. Organizations exist to help people make social and sexual contacts and if you have a disability, you may want to get in touch. ▨

TO FIND OUT MORE

Fat is a Feminist Issue, Susie Orbach, published by Arrow.
How do I look ? Jill Dawson, published by Virago.

♥ ♥ ♥ ♥ ♥

chapter ten

BABY TALK

For obvious reasons, this chapter is written mainly from the girl's point of view, but boys should read it too. It takes two people to make love and two to get pregnant.

HOW DO I KNOW IF I'M PREGNANT?

If you have had sex with penetration without using any contraception, or if a condom has burst, then it is possible you will get pregnant. If you don't want to be, and it's less than three days since you had sex, head straight to your doctor or clinic for emergency contraception. (See Chapter 6.)

Otherwise you need to wait and see if your period arrives. Of course, missing a period can be caused by other things - even the worry of thinking you may be pregnant. The only sure way of knowing is to have a pregnancy test. It's best to wait until a few days after your period should have arrived. That's why it's always wise to keep a note of your period dates in your diary.

You can have a pregnancy test free of charge at your doctor's or Family Planning Clinic. If you are under sixteen, it may be better to go to a clinic if you don't want your parents to know. Or you can buy a pregnancy testing kit from the chemist's. They are quite expensive and you need to follow the instructions very carefully. There are also private advice centres which offer tests for a fee which includes counselling.

YOUR TEST IS NEGATIVE

Phew! Be sure that you organize your birth control arrangements better in future if you don't want to get pregnant. You may not be so lucky next time.

YOUR TEST IS POSITIVE

This means that you are definitely pregnant. Assuming that you didn't plan to get pregnant, you now have some choices to make and the sooner the better. Take a deep breath and try not to panic. Like Kim, you may feel that you just want to hide yourself away and pretend it isn't happening. This is a really bad idea and will waste time. There is lots of help available and you need people to talk to and to give you support. Think about telling your boyfriend. He may not be as hopeless as Danny and it's his responsibility too. Bear in mind that he may be as shocked as you are and if you are under sixteen, he may be worried about breaking the law.

You need to sit down together and work out what to do. Is the relationship strong enough to cope with a baby? Is this the right time for you both? Do you have the resources to give a child a home? If you think you may go ahead and have the baby, you need to know what his attitude is and what help and support he will give. If he doesn't want to know, can you cope with adoption or bringing up the child on your own? You will also want his support if you decide to have an abortion. Sometimes the boy wants the girl to keep the baby, but she doesn't want to. Although it may seem unfair, the father has no rights over you or the baby.

You'll probably have to tell your parents in the end, especially if you are under sixteen and need their permission to have an abortion. So it's better to do it sooner rather than later. Most parents rally round once they get over the shock and want to help as best they can. Sometimes it's a good idea to speak to a family friend first, who can advise on the best way of approaching your parents

If you are at school or college and have a sympathetic teacher, it may be worth telling him or her. Your parents will be worried about your education if you decide to keep the baby, so a teacher could give you good advice.

Above all, remember that you are not the first person who has ever fallen pregnant by mistake. Whatever you do, don't run away - being homeless will make matters far worse. Don't bottle up your feelings either but talk to a good friend or a counsellor and remember that once you have decided what to do, you will feel better.

THE CHOICES

HAVING THE BABY

If you decide to keep the baby, no one can make you have an abortion or force you to give your baby up for adoption. Just think as carefully as you can because it is a decision which will have repercussions for a long time. Try to work out whether you are making a positive decision to keep the baby, or a negative decision not to have an abortion.

However traumatic it may seem to face the idea of abortion, taking on a nine month pregnancy, giving birth and caring for another human being is a very big step to take.

Having the baby adopted is also a traumatic and painful decision. You may decide on adoption now but discover you feel quite differently once your baby is born.

If you decide to have the baby on your own, you will have to make lots of practical decisions about where to live and how to support yourself and your child. There are organizations which can help you. △

If you are planning to live with the father and get married, you need parental consent if you are under eighteen. But don't be pressured into getting married if you are not sure. A baby can put a big strain on a relationship, especially when the parents are very young. But it can also be a source of joy and satisfaction.

HAVING AN ABORTION

If you decide that this isn't the right time to have a baby and you do not want your baby adopted, then you will decide on an abortion, or medical 'termination' of pregnancy. Each year, thousands of women in Britain choose this alternative and although it is never an easy option, many women feel it is preferable to bringing another unwanted child into the world. You should be aware of these points:

The abortion debate As you know, abortion is still a controversial subject. Some people, particularly those with certain religious beliefs, believe it is immoral to deny the unborn child or 'foetus' (pronounced 'feetus') the right to life. This so-called 'pro-life' group believes that abortion should only be allowed in very extreme circumstances.

Other women believe it is every woman's right to choose whether or not to have a baby and that it is every child's birthright to be wanted. These women, known as the 'pro-choice' group, have campaigned to make abortions freely available to women who want them. They don't believe that either the woman or child should suffer as a result of inadequate birth control and don't want to see a return to the days of dangerous 'back street' illegal abortions.

To decide how you feel, it's important to talk to someone. If you are going for a National Health Service abortion, talk to your doctor.

If you are under sixteen, you need the written consent of your parent or guardian, or social worker if you are in care. The private pregnancy advisory services also offer counselling before and after the abortion. Ⓐ

The law The law states that you can only get an abortion if two doctors sign a form saying that to continue being pregnant would mean a risk to the mental or physical health of yourself or other children in your family. It also allows abortion if there is evidence that your child will be born seriously handicapped or if you have the HIV virus that can cause AIDS. This gives a lot of discretion to the doctor, so it is important that you go to see your doctor as soon as possible. They may recommend you for an NHS abortion or may suggest you go to one of the private organizations listed at the end of this book.

If your doctor agrees to an NHS abortion, you will be referred to a specialist at your local hospital who will perform the operation. There are often delays involved and the availability and speed of getting an abortion can depend on where you live and the attitudes of the doctors involved.

Because of religious beliefs, abortion is not legal in Northern Ireland, and women there who want abortions have to travel to England for the operation. The Ulster Pregnancy Advisory Association will put you in touch with clinics in England. Ⓐ

Time limits Time is all important and the sooner the abortion is carried out, the simpler the procedure. Abortions can legally be carried out up to the twenty-fourth week of pregnancy, but most take place before the twelfth week, i.e. within twelve weeks of your last period. Abortions can be done safely later than this but it's a bigger operation and there needs to be a special reason.

Private abortions Abortions can be carried out privately through one of the non-profit-making charities, but they are still expensive (about £150 to £220). Agencies like the British Pregnancy Advisory Service will give you confidential advice and counselling and refer you to a clinic where you will be looked after by sympathetic staff. Their clinics are all over the country and you will usually have to stay overnight. They will also help you plan better birth control in future.

The procedure Most abortions involve a simple procedure under local or general anaesthetic known as vacuum aspiration: a small bendy tube is inserted up the vagina through the cervix into the womb. The other end is attached to a suction machine which gently draws out the contents of the womb. This only takes a few minutes. Afterwards you will bleed and may have some cramps rather like a heavy period. You will normally recover very quickly and will be allowed home after a few hours' rest or the next morning. You will probably be asked to return a few weeks later for a check up and birth control advice.

The aftermath The whole process of discovering you are pregnant and making the decision to have an abortion involves a lot of emotional strain. So although you may feel relieved to get the abortion over with and to know you aren't pregnant any more, don't be surprised if you also feel sad and depressed. This may happen straight after the abortion or later on, perhaps when the baby would have been born.

Remember too that your hormones will need time to get back to normal after a few weeks of pregnancy and as we saw in Chapter 2, this can play havoc with your emotions. As usual, the advice is not to bottle up your feelings but to talk them through with friends. If you would like 'post-abortion' counselling, the organizations already mentioned can arrange this.

♥ ♥ ♥ ♥ ♥

HEALTH CHECK

chapter eleven

HEALTH CHECK

One of the messages that keeps coming up is that you can't expect other people to like you if you don't like yourself. In other words, if you want to have loving relationships, you must love yourself first.

People with a really low opinion of themselves tend to have difficulty relating to others. Either they'll cling desperately to whoever they find, because they're so grateful to be loved, or they'll despise anyone who cares for them because they feel they're worth so little. Either way, you'll find it a lot easier to have a happy emotional life if you can feel proud of yourself and your identity.

One good way to take pride in yourself is to look after your mind and body. And that doesn't mean only doing something when you're ill. Being healthy isn't just the opposite of being ill: it's feeling positive about life and protecting your well being. You don't have to become a fanatical health freak either. Much of it is common sense. Here are the main things to keep in mind:

YOU ARE WHAT YOU EAT

Most young people don't have to worry too much about their diet, but if you want to feel healthy and energetic and keep your hair and skin in good condition:

■ Eat a good variety of nutritious foods, such as fresh fruit and vegetables, non-fatty meats, fish, wholemeal bread and fibre. Cutting down on sugar, sweet drinks and greasy food will help you keep in shape. Healthy eating doesn't have to be any more expensive than eating junk food, particularly if you learn to cook.

■ If you're a vegetarian, it's important to eat a wide variety of vegetables and pulses like beans, so that you get all the proteins your body needs. There are lots of good vegetarian cook books that suggest balanced meals.

■ Lots of young people, especially girls, worry about their weight, but very few young people are medically overweight. It's better to eat healthily and take regular exercise (walking and dancing are fine) rather than go on crash diets. Many eating problems are psychological and are described in the previous chapter.

CHECK OUT AND CHECK UP

Going for checkups is an important way of preserving your health and taking fast action if something is going wrong. Unfortunately the government makes people pay for some services which were once free, but try to go as often as you can:

Teeth There are few things more likely to make your life a misery and to put people off you than rotten teeth. Regular brushing and a visit to your dentist every six months will keep your teeth healthy now and help you keep your own teeth when you're older. Treatment is free if you are:

■ Under sixteen.

■ Under nineteen and in full-time education.

■ Drawing income support or family credit.

■ Pregnant or have a child under one year old.

■ On low income (see form D11 from your post office to check if you are eligible).

Eyes You don't need to put up with the inconvenience and headaches caused by poor eyesight. An eye test is quick and painless. Tests used to be free but now you will be charged about £10. If you need glasses, the optician who tested you will give you a prescription, but you can take it anywhere to buy the glasses. For more details, ask your local optician.

Cervical smear tests for women This is a very important test which can save a lot of women's lives. It involves taking a few loose cells from the cervix or neck of the womb, which is at the top of the vagina. These cells are sent to the laboratory and examined under a microscope to see if there are any abnormalities which might lead to illness, particularly cervical cancer. If you're over twenty or sexually active and haven't already had a smear test, you should go to your doctor or family planning clinic and discuss making an appointment.

It's important to have regular smear tests throughout your life - at least every three years. Cervical cancer can be cured easily if it's spotted early enough. (Most women who die of cervical cancer have never had a smear test.) The test is free on the NHS and is simple and painless.

If you do get a positive result, don't panic. Any abnormalities can be treated easily before they ever develop into cancer. An organization called The Women's National Cancer Control Campaign will give you more information about this and other women's health problems. ⬙

Breast cancer screening Breast cancer is rare in young women but is the main killer of older women. (Now closely rivaled by lung cancer.) The illness can be detected early by checking for lumps in your breast and this is something you can learn to do yourself. Ask your doctor or Family Planning Clinic for information about breast self-examination.

Testicular cancer checks Any inflammation, difficulty in peeing, discharge, swelling, lump, spot or pain in the penis or balls should be reported to your doctor as soon as you've noticed it.

ALTERNATIVE AND COMPLEMENTARY

So-called 'alternative' medicine emphasizes preventing illness by keeping the whole body healthy. Greater importance is put on treating the entire person rather than just treating symptoms. Alternative medicine like acupuncture, homeopathy and herbal remedies has a long history. Recently there has been increased interest, particularly among younger people, in these 'New Age' alternatives as a way of complementing the traditional Western approach. To find out more about what's available, contact the Institute for Complementary Medicine or the Society of Homeopaths. ⬙

MENTAL PROBLEMS

Mental illness can hit us or people close to us at any time in our lives, whether it takes the form of a period of depression, a nervous breakdown or a personality-changing condition like schizophrenia. Unfortunately, there is still a lot of prejudice against sufferers, but it's absurd to be ashamed of something so common. Since many of us may experience some kind of mental disturbance at some time, it's important to know what to do:

STRESS

Stress has become known as the twentieth century disease and is held responsible for many health problems from heart attacks to drug addiction and neurosis. But stress isn't all bad and we may need a certain amount of it in our lives to get us out of bed in the morning and to keep us alert.

The problems start when we have too much stress. Then we can become anxious, depressed or obsessional and suffer violent mood swings. We all have periods like this occasionally, so it's important to recognize stress and to know how to cope. Here are some classic symptoms of stress:

■ Feeling tense and irritable and flying off the handle easily.
■ Finding it difficult to get to sleep.
■ Having frequent indigestion and stomach or bowel complaints.
■ Having frequent mood swings.
■ Finding it difficult to concentrate or to relax.
■ Smoking and/or drinking more than usual.

If this sounds like you, and it's been going on for a while, there are a variety of ways to tackle stress. Some are better than others:

Booze and drugs Increasing the use of alcohol, nicotine and other drugs to escape the pressures of life is a common way to react to stress. It is also one of the worst. You might feel a temporary sense of release, but beware! You are much more likely to become addicted to something if you're using it at a time when you're not feeling in control of your life. You can get into a vicious circle of needing the drugs to escape from stress and then finding that the stress is made worse by the effects of the drugs.

Sex and exercise Exercise and sex can be very good ways of relaxing, but some people try to escape stress by doing both to extremes. Exercise in particular can become addictive because of the short-term high you get from it. It causes a chemical to be released into your blood which acts like a drug. You may end up wanting to do nothing except go to the gym, jog or do hours of aerobics. Like abusing drink or drugs, you are just replacing one problem with another.

Tranquillizers 'Tranx' like valium are sometimes prescribed if you're feeling really anxious or freaked out. A short course can be helpful in an emergency but don't continue to take them for more than a month. Doctors have been over-prescribing tranquillizers for years, particularly to depressed women. (They were known in the sixties as 'Mother's Little Helper'.)

As well as being seriously addictive, they work by suppressing your emotions and numbing feelings. This can make it more difficult to sort out the root of your problem. Tranquillizers often cause severe withdrawal symptoms when you stop taking them. Many people simply can't face living without their pills and remain addicts for years. If you want help coming off these pills, contact the self-help organization 'Tranx'. ◪

Relaxation therapies The best way to cope with stress is to learn to relax without using drugs. There are lots of ways to do this, ranging from sitting and listening to quiet music or going for a swim to learning special techniques like meditation or yoga. One of the latest methods is lying underwater in a flotation tank! You can learn some of these techniques from books or evening classes.

A simple way of beating stress is to rest your brain and body by sitting and breathing deeply with your eyes closed for ten minutes twice a day. Alternative therapies like acupuncture or hypnotherapy may also be useful. These treatments can be expensive, but some practitioners give cheaper rates for people without much money. Your local paper or health food shop may supply names and addresses.

Counselling Most stress comes from a particular life problem and it's far better to tackle that problem directly rather than pretend it doesn't exist. Some problems are too hard to tackle alone and that's where counselling can help. Counselling simply means talking your problem over with a stranger who is specially trained and experienced. Your counsellor will have no axe to grind, won't make you feel bad or judge you and will help you explore your options and make the right choices. There are many organizations which offer different kinds of counselling, some especially for younger people. You could also ask your doctor for counselling on the NHS, but this service is scarce. Unfortunately, doctors themselves don't have enough training in counselling and often prescribe pills like tranquillizers when counselling would be much more helpful. ◪

EATING PROBLEMS

About one in two hundred young women suffer from anorexia nervosa or bulimia, both serious eating disorders which can lead to death. Much fewer men have this problem. A long period of therapy may be needed to help the sufferer get over the deep-rooted problems which cause the illness. Contact the organization Anorexic Aid for help and see Chapter 10 for more information on eating problems. ◪

DEPRESSION

It's often thought that young people don't suffer from depression and their feelings are dismissed as being just 'a phase' or part of growing up. But people of all ages can suffer from depression and it can be a crippling condition. It is certainly worth getting help if you feel severely depressed for any length of time. (See Chapter 2 for more information.)

NERVOUS BREAKDOWNS

Some people find that life suddenly becomes too much for them and they simply cannot cope any more. This may be caused by a particular trauma or just a gradual build-up of stress until they reach the breaking point. The term 'nervous breakdown' or 'cracking-up' is a very vague term and covers a wide variety of problems. Some people withdraw into themselves and stop going out or eating and taking care of themselves. Others may become manic and obsessional, unable to rest or communicate normally. Often family and friends will be the first to notice that something's wrong and a period of rest and recovery, with expert help and support, will be needed.

SCHIZOPHRENIA

Schizophrenia affects just under one in a hundred people. Despite its name, schizophrenia doesn't really mean split personality. Symptoms may include a whole range of false beliefs and delusions about the world and other people, a difficulty in thinking rationally and an inability to express emotions.

This illness can be very frightening. It puts a huge strain on the sufferer as well as family and friends. It's important to seek help as soon as possible. Your GP should be contacted first and the local Social Services should help with day centres, housing or workshop schemes. The National Schizophrenia Fellowship provides information about the illness and runs a national network of support groups for sufferers and carers. ◪

COPING WITH ILLNESS AND DEATH

Coping with serious illness, your own or affecting someone you love, can put a great strain on everyone involved. Although each person's experience is unique, one of the best ways of getting support is to discuss it with people who have gone through similar problems. This is also true if you have to cope with the death of someone close to you.

As well as coming to terms with your own feelings of grief and loss, you may have to deal with practical changes - so do seek help and don't take the British 'stiff upper lip' approach. Putting on a brave face and bottling up your feelings is not the best way of coping. Try to express how you feel and if you need someone to talk to, contact CRUSE, an organization for bereaved people. They've recently set up a section for younger people. ◪

DRUG USE AND ABUSE

People use drugs for many different reasons, some medical, some social. Many take drugs because they like the mood-changing effects such as the lift you get from the caffeine in coffee to get you going in the morning. Some drugs are legal, like tobacco and alcohol. Others are illegal. The one thing they have in common is that it's easy to get hooked on these substances and too much of any drug can damage your health and even ruin your life.

Understandably, young people often feel they're constantly preached at about the dangers of something they see as being just good fun. They also resent the double standards of a society which allows the use of a dangerous drug like alcohol (and collects a huge amount of money from taxes) while condemning other less dangerous drugs. But preaching aside, it's worth knowing as much as you can about different drugs and their effects so that you can make choices and know what you might be letting yourself in for.

If you do use drugs and inject them and share needles, there's a very high chance of catching the HIV virus which causes AIDS.

LEGAL DRUGS

S m o k i n g This is becoming less popular, but a lot of young people, girls in particular, are still smoking. There is no doubt at all that smoking damages your health. It makes you less fit from the time you start and can kill you in the end. It's also expensive and very addictive. The best way to stop is never to start because the nicotine in tobacco is so addictive. If you want to give it up, there are organizations like ASH which can help, or do it together with a group of friends. ◪

Alcohol It's part of our everyday lives and the odd drink or two does no harm. But it is a powerful and dangerous drug and even drinking a small amount of alcohol will slow down your reactions and can cause accidents. Never drink and drive. Lots of people damage their health by drinking too much, even if they're not alcoholics.

So how much is too much? Experts agree that you are probably damaging your health if you drink more than:

■ Women: 12-14 units per week.
■ Men: 20-22 units per week.

One unit = half a pint of ordinary beer or lager = single measure of spirits = one glass of wine.

It's all too easy to become dependent on alcohol, and if you feel you've got a problem go to your doctor or contact your local Alcoholics Anonymous branch. If someone close to you has an alcohol problem, you can contact Al-Anon, which is a support group for relatives of alcoholics. Al-Ateen is a group for young people with drink problems themselves or for those who have a drink problem in their families. ◪

Solvents and glue These generally produce excitement and loss of control, hallucinations, risk of choking on vomit, risk of serious heart and brain damage and dependence. They can cause sudden death.

Amyl nitrate (poppers) Used as a muscle relaxant, poppers speed up the heartbeat. Popular among gay men and clubbers. Have been known to cause instantaneous brain and heart damage.

ILLEGAL DRUGS

A m p h e t a m i n e s (speed, fast, wizz) White or brown powder usually sniffed ('snorted'), but can be swallowed or injected. Makes people lively, distractable and alert, but depression, dependence and panic can follow. Speed is addictive and can certainly damage your health.

C a n n a b i s (pot, dope, hash, grass, blow, shit, weed) Smoked in a joint or pipe. Causes feelings of relaxation and intoxication but can also make people feel weird or paranoid. Although it is not physically addictive or harmful to health, you can become dependent on it and waste your life in a stoned haze.

C o c a i n e (coke) A white powder, usually sniffed. Effects similar to speed, elation followed by depression. To avoid the depression some people take more and more coke and start the cycle of addiction. People often drink and smoke more on coke.

H e r o i n (smack, junk, H, skag) White or speckled brown powder. Can be inhaled, sniffed or injected. It slows down bodily functions and produces feelings of euphoria but you need larger and larger amounts after a short time. Coming off it once you're hooked can be unpleasant, so lots of people stay addicts. It can produce personality changes after a while and often leads to criminal activity in order to support the habit.

L S D (acid) Tiny coloured tablets taken by mouth. Can cause personality changes, hallucinations, panic, ideas of persecution and can lead to long term mental disorder.

P s i l o c y b i n (m a g i c   m u s h r o o m s) Tiny mushrooms eaten fresh or dried. They grow wild in the UK. Effects and risks are similar to LSD, plus there is the risk of eating poisonous mushrooms by mistake.

MDMA or ecstasy ('E', disco biscuit) Cross between a hallucinogenic drug and speed. Can cause serious physical and mental side effects. It is a recent drug and there's a danger of 'fake' versions, so you can't be exactly sure of what you're taking. This is true of many drugs sold illegally.

Crack A mixture of cocaine, baking powder and water in white crystals. Effects similar to coke but stronger, more rapid and short lived. It can cause almost immediate dependence.

Barbiturates (downers) Prescribed as sleeping pills. Produce lack of feeling and lack of co-ordination. Addictive - with very bad withdrawal symptoms.

GETTING OFF DRUGS

Although many people experiment with drugs without becoming addicted, many others find that the use of legal or illegal drugs and their mood-changing effects become habit forming. This leads to severe problems. Apart from the health risks involved with particular substances, the cycle of addiction can end up dominating your entire life. Love and relationships, work and pleasure can all fade into insignificance compared with the need to maintain the habit. Sadly, many addicts report that they end up continuing to take the drug not because they get anything positive from it but because they just can't do without it.

However, lots of people do give up successfully, and if you have a problem, there are people who have gone through it before you and can help. Many organizations give support and counselling, and a few residential centres provide a place to start rebuilding your life. The first step is to face up to the problem and not be afraid to seek help. ◭

GETTING WHAT YOU WANT

A lot of people have a good idea of what they want and how to look after themselves but still end up not doing it. All of us from time to time let ourselves be talked into doing things that we know aren't in our interests, but if it happens too often we may have a problem. 'Why did I let myself do it?' The answer is usually that people don't have the self-confidence and the skills to assert themselves and say 'no'. Or they don't know how to suggest an alternative they would prefer. Here are a variety of different situations in which people have difficulty either saying 'no' or suggesting alternatives:

■ Having your hair cut the way you want it rather than the way the hairdresser wants to do it.
■ Being given drugs or booze you don't really want.
■ Putting up with sexual harassment at work or college.
■ Not feeling able to ask for a pay rise or to change your course at college.
■ Being persuaded to have sex when you don't want to.
■ Not feeling able to tell your partner what you like sexually or how you'd like to change your sex life, e.g. practising safer sex.
■ Not feeling able to end a relationship which isn't making you happy.

TRAINING AND CHANGING

If you want to make positive choices, you must learn to be more assertive. Being assertive isn't the same as being aggressive. It's stating what you want clearly and calmly and not giving in to pressure from others or feeling guilty about asking for what you want.

If you feel you'd benefit from some assertiveness training, there are now several books on the subject. Ask at your local library. These books will explain techniques to help you change your behaviour so that you are more likely to get what you want.

You can also learn this in assertiveness training classes. Some classes are for women only, since many women still suffer from society's expectation that women should take the passive role. In these classes, you will be taught skills of assertiveness and be able to practise them with other people in the class.

Here are some principles of assertiveness training:

Persistence You will be taught to swop your usual habit of silently letting someone else get their own way, with standing up for yourself. Without being aggressive or getting angry, you will be taught to repeat your demands to someone. You won't let this person beat you down by saying 'no' or changing the subject. You will learn the art of outnumbering your opponent's 'no's'.

Realistic compromises In situations of conflict, one solution is to suggest options which will satisfy both you and the other person. You will be taught how to suggest these compromises in ways which maintain your self-respect.

Coping with criticism People often give up on what they want because they are desperate to be liked and can't bear criticism. The best way to handle unpleasant criticism from others is to hear them out, while still sticking to what you want.

Encouraging others to be assertive rather than aggressive When people are criticizing something you are doing, they are often hinting at more than they are saying. If you learn to ask them to explain what they mean by their criticism, this will have two effects: you'll be less likely to buckle under the hidden pressure, and others will learn to be more open with you instead of trying to manipulate you.

TO FIND OUT MORE

Compulsion, Eleanor Stephens and Robin Blake, published by Boxtree.

Coming off Drugs, James and Joyce Ditzler, published by Macmillan.

MORE
SEX TALK

chapter twelve

MORE
SEX TALK

It's good that Kim and Danny are talking to their friends about how they feel about sex, but they really need to talk to each other. Making love is all about communication and finding out what you both enjoy. You cannot expect to know how to please your partner immediately and lovers are not telepathic, whatever the romantic myths may suggest. It's important to take the time and have the confidence to discuss with each other what pleases you both.

Too many couples never talk openly about sex to one another, and as a result they get into a habit of having sex which isn't as satisfying as it could be. The needs of one partner may often be neglected and this can cause resentment, storing up problems for the future.

Making love involves trust and sharing, and most sexual problems can be sorted out with some straight talking. You also need the confidence to explore alternatives to find out what each of you really enjoys.

Don't think of sex as some kind of performance in which you have to prove yourself. The old-fashioned image of the man as a 'macho stud' is disappearing but people may still feel pressures on them to perform. There is no one right way to have sex. Part of the pleasure of lovemaking is the diversity and variety involved. The only correct way to have sex is to do whatever gives you and your partner the most pleasure - and you need to talk to each other to find that out.

HOW TO TALK ABOUT SEX

If you are starting a sexual relationship or want to change certain aspects of your sex life with your partner, there are good and bad ways of discussing sex. How and when you choose to talk about it will depend on the way that you both communicate but here are some suggestions:

After sex It is probably not a good idea to discuss what you don't enjoy about sex immediately afterwards, as your partner may feel that they have exposed their feelings to you and that your criticisms are a slap in the face. If you are feeling frustrated because you're not getting enough out of it, you may just sound angry. This will not help you to communicate or get the best response from your partner.

During an argument It is quite common for couples to bring up lots of irritations during a row about something completely different. Often someone will say, 'And when it comes to sex, you always...' then list their partner's defects. Try to avoid this kind of confrontation as it will only create more barriers between you.

Over a meal This is a much better situation in which to discuss your sex life, particularly if you already enjoy making love and and just want to experiment some more. But if you want to make drastic changes, it can seem cold and clinical to talk about how you should be having sex in a non-sexual situation. Your partner may find it embarrassing and it could put you both off your meal!

Before and during sex A good time to talk about what you want is just before and during sex. Think about what you want your partner to do that they are not doing already and think about how you could both change your usual pattern of lovemaking. Don't feel shy about making suggestions - it's a sign that you care about what happens between you and talking about sex can be erotic too. If your partner takes no notice and just carries on regardless, don't just scream at them to stop. Put your criticism in a positive way: 'That feels good, but it would feel even better if you did it this way'.

Don't feel embarrassed to guide your partner's hand and show him or her exactly how you want to be touched. (This is particularly important for women who are not getting the kind of clitoral stimulation they need to have an orgasm.) The main point to bear in mind when you're talking about lovemaking is not to make the other person feel as if they are being got at or that you don't fancy them or love them any more. (Unless this is true.) Try to get across that it's because you care about them that you want your lovemaking to be as pleasurable as possible with no one feeling left out.

PROBLEMS WITH ORGASMS

Some of the most common sex problems revolve around orgasms. Many, perhaps most, people find at some time in their lives that orgasms don't just happen as they want. There are a variety of different problems, but usually one solution: discussing it with your partner and experimenting with different ways of making love.

WOMEN

Unable to have an orgasm Many women find that they don't come during sex even if they can reach an orgasm easily through masturbation. There can be several reasons for this:

■ Her partner may not be giving her the right kind of stimulation or carrying on long enough. Most women need regular stimulation of the clitoris and vaginal penetration on its own doesn't provide this. If you masturbate, you will probably know what is going wrong so share this knowledge with your partner. Most partners will want to learn to please you, so don't feel shy. A few men may resent such suggestions. In that case, you should persist or find another partner. Either way, it's his problem not yours.

■ Perhaps a male partner isn't aware of the function of the woman's clitoris at all. You must point it out to him and explain that it is very similar to the penis in terms of responsiveness. Explain clearly what you want him to do and the kind of rhythm and pressure you enjoy.

■ Many women would like to touch themselves either before, during or after intercourse, but feel too embarrassed. Explain to your partner that this helps you enjoy lovemaking more and leaves his hands free to explore other erogenous zones. In general, your partner is sure to be turned on more if you are.

■ Many women feel overwhelmed by the pressure to come and this blocks off their responses and stops it happening. Think of your orgasm as being for yourself, as and when you want it. Making love isn't a performance or a competition and you need not feel a failure if you don't come. Take it easy and you're more likely to come when you want. If your partner keeps insisting that you must come, don't fake an orgasm. Faking orgasm is unfair to yourself and your partner and will only store up problems for the future. Explain that putting pressure on you is only making it worse. If this problem persists and you feel you can't let go, you might want to talk to a counsellor.

■ Some women only have sex when their partner wants it, not when they want it. So it's no wonder they aren't turned on enough to reach a climax. Making love should be mutual, so take the initiative when you really feel like it and don't be bullied.

MEN

There are some problems men have with orgasm:

Premature ejaculation Many men come much more quickly than either they or their partner would like. They may ejaculate just as the penis has entered the vagina or a few seconds later. This is called 'premature ejaculation' and is particularly common in younger men.

It is often caused by tension and worry and it may get worse the more you think about it. Sometimes just talking to your partner about your anxiety makes it go away. If that doesn't work, you might find that the so-called 'squeeze method' will work.

Ask your partner to bring you close to orgasm by manual stimulation. When you feel you are about to come, get your partner to squeeze your penis firmly just below the head for about four seconds. This will make it slightly less erect and delay the orgasm. Repeat this several times so that you begin to control the sensations. Don't attempt penetration until you are used to this way of regaining control. Eventually confidence should return and this procedure become unnecessary. Many couples have used this method successfully and find that it can be pleasurable in itself as well as improving their communication about sex.

Retarded ejaculation Some men, though much fewer than mentioned above, find that it takes an uncomfortably long time to come or that they can't come at all. This is usually connected with a fear of letting go. Again, discussing it with your partner may help you to relax but if not, you may want to speak to your doctor about it.

In the end, whether you are masturbating or making love with a partner, enjoying it is all that matters. Many people don't need or want to have an orgasm every time they have sex. Everyone is different and you've only got a problem if you feel you have one. Don't listen to people who boast about coming five times a night or having multiple or simultaneous orgasms. It's your body and your sexuality so just relax and enjoy it.

DIFFERENT POSITIONS

Too many people think that lovemaking is just about penetration, often in what's called 'the missionary position': the woman lies on her back like an upturned beetle with the man heaving away on top! (This position got its name because interfering nineteenth-century Christian missionaries told Africans that this was the civilized position for intercourse.)

Many people really enjoy having sex in this position but there are lots of other ways of making love. And sex doesn't have to involve penetration at all. Touching, stroking, licking and rubbing are all expressions of desire which can be just as erotic whether or not they lead to intercourse and orgasm. So don't be afraid to ring the changes and experiment.

TO FIND OUT MORE

You may pick up some tips from some of the many sex manuals available, ranging from the *Kama Sutra* to the *Joy of Sex,* by Alex Comfort, published by Quartet. Some of them are more likely to make you laugh than to make you feel sexy but a sense of humour is a crucial ingredient in enjoying sex!

♥ ♥ ♥ ♥ ♥

SEX-RELATED DISEASES

chapter thirteen

SEX-RELATED DISEASES

A sexually transmitted disease (STD) is the name given to any disease which is mainly spread through sexual contact. (They used to be known as venereal diseases or VD.) Anyone who has sex can catch a sexually transmitted disease. You certainly don't have to be a particular 'type of person'. It's not your fault if you get an STD, any more than if you get the flu. The important thing is to seek medical treatment as quickly as possible and be sure you don't pass it on. Most STDs are easily cured but can cause a lot of damage if they are left untreated. So don't panic – follow Yvonne's lead and get down to that clinic!

WHAT ARE THE SYMPTOMS?

■ Discharge from the vagina or penis (not to be confused with the normal slight discharge which all women have). Unusually thick, cloudy or smelly discharge could indicate an STD such as thrush or gonorrhoea.

■ Itching, rashes, sores or irritation around the genitals and anus (arsehole).

■ Feeling as though you need to pee frequently and/or pain and burning when peeing. Blood in your urine.

■ Pain when you are having sex.

■ A feeling of being slightly unwell may accompany any of these symptoms.

WHAT TO DO ?

Yvonne was right to head straight off to her nearest special clinic. The doctors and health workers there specialize in these problems. They give confidential, free advice and treatment and you don't need a letter from your doctor. You can find their address in the phone book or call your local hospital. There are lots of different names for these clinics including: Special Clinic or STD Clinic; Department of Venereology.

If possible, go to the clinic with your partner. If you do have an infection then you may both need treatment. Don't be embarrassed – they see hundreds of people like you each week. It's better not to go during your period as some of the tests won't work then. It's good to make a list of your symptoms and the questions you want to ask so you don't forget anything when you see the doctor.

WHAT WILL HAPPEN AT THE CLINIC?

Your clinic visit may well take an hour or more, so take something to read. Once you've filled in some forms (all confidential) you will then be taken into the examination room for some tests. They will usually include:

■ A blood test. (They won't test for HIV virus unless you especially ask for this.)

■ Samples will be taken of tiny cells from the penis and the vagina to check for infections. For women, this means an internal examination: you lie on your back on the examining table, bend your legs up so that the doctor can look inside your vagina using a speculum. This is a metal or plastic object which holds the walls of your vagina apart. They may do a cervical smear at the same time to make sure that your cervix (the neck of the womb high up in the vagina) is healthy. (See Chapter 11.) This is quick and not painful.

■ You will probably be asked to pee into a small container so they can check your urine for bacteria. So don't pee just before seeing the doctor!

RESULTS

When you see the doctor you may get some results straight away. Or they may have to wait a week or so for your test results and so you will make an appointment to return. The doctor will explain what's wrong and what treatment you need. If you need pills such as a course of antibiotics, these will be given to you at the clinic. Be sure you understand what you have to do and don't be afraid to ask as many questions as you wish. Doctors are human too – they even have sex!

It's important that once you have spotted a possible symptom of infection, you don't have sex until you've been checked out at the clinic and finished your treatment. Be sure your partner gets treated too or you'll just pass the infection backwards and forwards between you.

If the clinic suggests you contact past sexual partners, it's sensible to follow their advice. Some clinics may offer to contact the people themselves, if you don't want to get in touch personally. They will be very discreet and won't give your name. Don't be embarrassed about this. You are really doing your contacts a big favour because they may not have any symptoms themselves. It can be very serious to leave STDs untreated.

PREVENTION

There are lots of ways to minimize the risk of catching STDs:

■ Always practise safer sex and if you have intercourse with penetration, use a condom. Condoms don't just prevent the spread of the HIV virus - they stop other diseases being passed on as well. (See Chapter 5.)

■ Keep your genitals clean and wash before and after sex if possible. Peeing soon after sex can also flush out some of the germs which can cause infection. Always wipe yourself from the front to the back so germs from the anus won't get into the vagina or the urethra.
■ Don't have sex with someone who has any sores or rashes around their genitals and don't let someone with cold sores kiss your genitals.

Avoid painful intercourse and use plenty of lubrication such as KY jelly or spermicide.

■ Don't go in for sex play that breaks the skin or french kiss if either of you has severely bleeding gums or mouth ulcers.

■ Avoid tight trousers and wear cotton rather than nylon pants. Hot, moist air encourages the bacteria to grow.

■ Avoid scented soaps, bath oils, talcs or vaginal deodorants which may contain chemicals that irritate the delicate skin around your genitals.

■ Look after your body with good food and rest so that you can fight infections. (See Chapter 11.)

Finally, the more sexual partners you have, and the more partners your partner has, the more likely you are to catch something. Draw your own conclusions!

SEXUALLY TRANSMITTED DISEASES (STDs) AND OTHER ILLNESSES AFFECTING SEX ORGANS
(in alphabetical order)

A I D S   This is the most serious of all STDs and we have given it a separate chapter – Chapter 5.

C h l a m y d i a   This is the most common STD. While not serious in itself, if left untreated it can lead to a much more serious illness in women called pelvic inflammatory disease, which may result in infertility. Women often get no symptoms, or they may have some discharge from the vagina. If left untreated in males it can cause NSU (see Gardnerella). Males may get a discharge from the penis. Both may feel some pain when peeing and some irritation or soreness in the vagina or penis. If you have chlamydia, then your partner probably has too, so you should both take the antibiotics which cure it.

C y s t i t i s   Cystitis isn't a sexually transmitted disease, but it can be brought on by the friction involved with sex, particularly if you're not used to it. That's why it used to be known as the honeymoon disease. Cystitis is an infection of the bladder that affects many young women. Symptoms include:

■ Suddenly having to pee every few minutes, accompanied by burning sensations when you do.
■ Wanting to pee often without much coming out.
■ Blood or pus in the urine.

If any of these symptoms lasts for more than a few days you should see your doctor. But there are some self–help remedies for minor infections:

■ Drink lots of water, several glasses every hour.
■ Females should keep the bacteria from their anus away from the vagina by always wiping front to back.

■ Have two or three baths a day, and wash your genitals with a mild soap.

■ Take vitamin C regularly.

Gardnerella This is sometimes called non-specific vaginitis in a woman, or non-specific urethritis (NSU) in a man. It isn't always sexually transmitted. Women get a heavy, greyish, fishy-smelling discharge from the vagina or there may be no symptoms at all. Men seldom get any symptoms, or they may feel some soreness when peeing. Treat with antibiotics.

Hepatitis The viruses causing hepatitis A and hepatitis B can be transmitted sexually as well as through other methods (especially sharing needles for drugs). The virus is found in the sufferer's faeces (shit) and so is likely to be transmitted by anal intercourse and oral sex that involves the mouth coming into contact with the anus. It is a serious illness that attacks the liver and causes nausea, vomiting, jaundice and sometimes permanent liver damage. The illness can't be cured, but a doctor can give injections of hepatitis B vaccine to the partner of someone who is carrying the virus.

Genital herpes You get herpes from contact with someone who has a herpes sore. (It's estimated that at least 50 per cent of people have the virus.) If your partner has a sore on the genitals, then you could get it from intercourse. It is more usual for the herpes virus to get to the genital area by oral sex. The first attack of herpes is usually the worst. A really painful red blister-like sore appears on the vagina, vulva, penis or anal area. There may also be flu-like symptoms. Subsequent attacks are a lot milder, and they often become less frequent until they just stop altogether. There is no cure for herpes, although doctors can prescribe a medicine called Acyclovir.

Genital warts These are spread by anal or vaginal sex or from fingers to the genitals. They tend to be reddish-pink, painless little cauliflower-like growths. Small ones are treated with a special lotion or cream. Larger ones have to be burnt or frozen off. This is painless.

Gonorrhoea Also known as 'the clap' or 'a dose'. It can only be caught through intercourse with penetration. In women there can be no symptoms at all or a burning feeling when peeing and a yellowish discharge from the vagina. They may also get a fever and achy flu-like symptoms. Men's symptoms are similar with a yellowish discharge from the penis. Treatment is with antibiotics and it's important to go back to the clinic to find out if you're clear.

Pelvic inflammatory disease (PID) This is a serious disease for women, usually caused by leaving other diseases like chlamydia and gonorrhoea untreated for too long. It can lead to a woman becoming infertile. PID causes general feelings of tiredness, fever, pains in the lower part of the abdomen and the back, an abnormal discharge, heavy or irregular periods, nausea and/or vomiting and pain during intercourse. Antibiotics can cure PID in its early stages, but if it is left until late, infected organs may have to be removed.

Pubic lice Also known as crabs or nits. These little creatures live in the pubic hair and feed on your blood. They look like little brown dots at the roots of your hairs and itch fiercely. You can catch crabs from close physical contact with someone who has them, or from bedding, shared clothes, towels or even a loo seat which has just been used by someone with crabs. Use a special lotion to kill the lice, like Prioderm. You can get it from a chemist without a prescription. Re-use after fourteen days.

Syphilis Sometimes called the pox, this is very serious if left untreated. It can only be caught through sex with penetration. In the first stage, a sore develops near or on the vagina or penis. In the second, a copper-coloured skin rash develops anywhere on the body and the sufferer gets flu-like symptoms. Finally, the disease, if untreated, will lead to paralysis, blindness, madness and eventually death. It's easy to cure with antibiotics.

Thrush Its medical name is candida albicans. This is a common complaint and not usually transmitted through sex. It can be caused by antibiotics. For girls, thrush produces a thick white vaginal discharge which looks like cottage cheese and smells yeasty. It causes severe vaginal itching and is painful when you pee. In boys it can cause soreness under the foreskin. The doctor will prescribe tablets or a special cream.

Trichomoniasis (Also known as 'trich') is a small parasite that can infect men and women. It's passed on during intercourse and causes a foul-smelling green or greyish vaginal discharge. It can be treated with pills and cream.

TO FIND OUT MORE

Our Bodies, Ourselves, Angela Phillips and Jill Rakusen, published by Penguin.

chapter fourteen

SEX AND
THE LAW

Laws on sex are about as confused and illogical as many people's attitudes on the subject. Some of them positively protect people, like the law against child abuse. But others, like laws about homosexuality, seem designed to punish. Whether you intend to keep them, break them or change them, it is important to know what they are.

HETEROSEXUAL AGE OF CONSENT

Laws on straight sex are generally designed to protect girls from the sexual advances of boys and men:

■ It's illegal for a boy/man to have any sexual contact with a girl under sixteen (seventeen in Northern Ireland, eighteen in the Republic of Ireland).

■ A boy under fourteen cannot be charged with 'unlawful sexual intercourse' or with rape.

■ If you and your girlfriend live together and she is under sixteen, you could be charged with taking an unmarried girl away from her parents, even if you don't have sex.

■ Women can only be charged with indecent assault on a boy under sixteen, not with 'unlawful sexual intercourse'.

■ It's illegal for a man to have anal intercourse with a woman at any age.

HOMOSEXUAL AGE OF CONSENT
AND OTHER LAWS

The law discriminates against homosexuality but it attacks gay men and lesbians differently. For example, lesbian mothers often have their children taken away from them after court battles, while the law attacks gay men's sexuality:

■ Lesbian relationships have never been illegal, partly because heterosexuals used not to believe that two women could have a sexual relationship. So if both women are over sixteen, the relationship is legal.

■ It is illegal for men to have a sexual relationship with a boy or a man unless you are both twenty-one or over. The relationship is then only legal if it takes place between two consenting individuals in private with both consenting, and provided you are not in the armed forces. All gay male sex is illegal in the armed forces.

■ If you are caught having sex with another man in a public place, you may be charged with gross indecency, an offence which doesn't exist for straights, or with importuning.

AIDS AND YOUR RIGHTS

■ No one can be tested for HIV if they don't want to be. This applies to all young people including those in care or in custody.

■ If you decide to be tested you have the right to pre-test counselling and you must be able to give your 'informed consent' to the test. (See Chapter 5.)

MARRIAGE AND LIVING TOGETHER

■ You can't marry until you're sixteen, but Max is right that he doesn't need parental consent over eighteen.

■ If you're sixteen or seventeen and want to marry, you need the written permission of your parents or guardian. If they refuse, you can go to court.

■ If you're under eighteen and your parents or guardian object to you living with your boy/girlfriend, they can take you to court, and you could legally be taken into care.

YOUR RIGHTS ON CONTRACEPTION
AND ABORTION

■ If you're under sixteen and want advice on birth control without your parents knowing, the doctor or clinic will probably co-operate, but can legally refuse.

■ Aged sixteen or over, you are entitled to advice on birth control without anyone else's consent. Contraceptives from the Family Planning Clinics or on prescription are free.

■ In the Republic of Ireland it is illegal to advise or prescribe contraception for unmarried people.

■ An abortion needs the consent of two doctors. (See Chapter 7.) If you are under sixteen, the law requires your doctor to inform your parents. Don't let this stop you from seeking advice as soon as possible.

RAPE AND INDECENT ASSAULT

■ A man or boy aged fourteen or over who has sexual intercourse with a girl/woman who does not consent, has committed rape. Rape is legally defined as the penis penetrating the vagina.

■ It is not consent if she says 'yes' as a result of threats or drugs.

■ If a man forces sexual acts on a woman against her will, which do not involve the penis penetrating the vagina, e.g. anal or oral sex, he can be charged with indecent assault or grievous bodily harm.

■ If a man penetrates another boy/man against his will, this is 'unlawful buggery', not rape.

DO YOU REPORT RAPE ?

Rape is a serious crime of violence and should be reported to the police so that the rapist can be caught and prevented from harming others. But there are many reasons why some women prefer not to report a rape; it is a very frightening experience and you may want to pretend it hasn't happened. But even if you decide not to report it, you should consider seeking help and support at a Rape Crisis Centre. These centres will also give you support if you do want to report the rape.

Some women don't report rape because they are worried they will be badly treated by the police and made to feel the crime is partly their fault. This used to happen often, but police attitudes have improved recently. Don't wash or change your clothes. Take a friend with you to the police station to give you moral support and take a change of clothing in case the police want to keep some of your clothes for evidence. You may have to have a medical examination. You can ask for a woman doctor and for your friend to be present.

Don't be surprised if it takes some time to get over such a bad experience. It often helps to talk to a counsellor about your feelings, and the Rape Crisis Centre will tell you how to arrange this. In order to regain your confidence, you may want to check the security of your home and learn how to defend yourself on the street. Many councils run self-defence courses and there are books on this subject.

◪

INCEST AND SEXUAL ABUSE

■ It is illegal to marry or have sexual intercourse with your father, mother, stepfather, stepmother, grandmother, grandfather, uncle, aunt, half-brother, half-sister, brother or sister.

■ Sexual acts which wouldn't be defined as sexual intercourse, for instance rubbing the genitals or having oral sex, are not classified as incest but are also illegal. They would be defined as indecent assault.

■ Some adults who are not blood relations, but are in parent-like positions, such as teachers, your mother's live-in boyfriend, etc. cannot be prosecuted for incest. They can be charged with indecent assault and/or rape.

UNDERSTANDING SEXUAL ABUSE

Recently it's become plain that many more young people than were previously thought (both boys and girls) are victims of sexual abuse. A recent poll found that 12 per cent of women and 8 per cent of men had had an abusive experience before the age of sixteen.

The laws covering rape and indecent assault, as well as those covering incest, can all be applied in cases of sexual abuse. But an enormous number of cases of sexual abuse are not reported. It is, therefore, necessary for young people to understand what sexual abuse is and how to deal with it.

Recognizing sexual abuse Abuse can range from children being cuddled or bathed in a way that makes them feel uncomfortable, to being forced to listen to sexual talk or actually being penetrated. The key factor in cases of child sexual abuse is that an older person is using a child in a sexual way. By virtue of being bigger, stronger, with more power and authority, the adult can persuade or force the child to have sexual experience.

The difference between abuse and children's sex play It's perfectly normal and healthy for children to play with their own and other children's bodies and genitals. There is no element of force in in these situations. Parents cuddling, playing or bathing with their children is also healthy and loving.

Boys can be victims too It used to be thought that very few boys were abused in comparison with girls. But it now appears that the problem is nearly as great for boys as it is for girls. Girls find that if they tell someone about abuse, they may not be believed and for boys this problem is much greater. The vast majority of boys who are abused never tell anyone, with the result that they may develop serious emotional problems later on in life.

Women rarely abuse There are very few cases of women abusing boys or men. Ninety-seven per cent of abusers are men.

Different kinds of abuse Abuse can occur as a one-off incident such as a rape by a stranger or a 'dirty' phone-call. Or it can take place over a number of years, with a neighbour, family friend or relative taking advantage of their closeness to and power over the child.

Why not tell? Children are taught to trust and obey adults and abusers use this to try to convince the child that their behaviour is normal. They may also win their silence by threatening them with the consequences of telling. Young people may feel that it is their fault they are abused, just as rape victims often blame themselves. Abuse is never the fault of the victim.

Why have I been abused? Most victims ask themselves this question. The answer is that anyone can be abused. There is no character type: you were just unlucky enough to be in the wrong place at the wrong time. It is not your fault.

What can I do? If you are currently being abused, you must tell someone about it as soon as possible. Tell someone that you trust or telephone a help line. ◮ Get in touch with a group through which you can meet other people in a similar situation. Eventually you may get the strength to report the incident to the police. This is important, as abusers tend to abuse and abuse again. Even if the abuse has now stopped, it is still vital for you talk about your feelings and not to bottle them up. You may need a period of counselling to get over these damaging experiences.

PROSTITUTION

Prostitution means selling sex for money and it is not actually illegal. However:

■ You can be arrested if you are soliciting to meet customers. The same laws apply to men and women who are prostitutes.

■ It is illegal to 'live off immoral earnings'. This means that anyone who runs a brothel, or who lives off the money a prostitute makes (known as a 'pimp'), can be prosecuted.

TO FIND OUT MORE

Take a Firm Stand: The Young Woman's Guide to Self-Defence, Vicky Grosser, Gaby Mason and Rani Parmar, published by Virago.

Out In The Open: A Guide for Young People Who Have Been Sexually Abused, Ouaine Bain and Maureen Sanders, published by Virago.

♥ ♥ ♥ ♥ ♥

CONCLUSION

One reason why people of all ages sometimes feel unhappy with their lives is because they feel powerless and not in control. Apart from our legal rights, we all have personal rights which we should stand up for as individuals and within relationships. We have mentioned them again and again throughout this book. They include the right:

- to ask for information and know our options
- to make our own choices
- to define our own sexuality and our own ways of loving
- to make mistakes and change our minds
- not to feel pressured into decisions and to ask for more time
- to ask for what we need and to negotiate our needs with others
- to express our feelings and to find sympathetic support

All the organizations listed in the next few pages can provide information, advice and support, so don't be afraid to contact them. It's always better to take action as soon as possible, rather than hoping that the problems will go away. Leaving them usually makes them worse.

So forget the old saying: 'Ignorance is bliss'. Substitute instead **'Knowledge is strength'** and with a sense of humour, you should be able not just to survive these important years, but to have some fun too.

♥ ♥ ♥ ♥ ♥

WHERE TO
GET HELP

△

These groups and organizations are listed in alphabetical order of subject. To contact them, either give them a ring or send a stamped addressed envelope. If you have difficulty contacting any of them, either contact a similar-sounding one or ask your local Citizens Advice Bureau (telephone number in book.)

ABORTION - see Contraception.

AIDS/HIV- INFECTION
For information
and advice on all aspects of AIDS/HIV
infection contact:
The Terrence Higgins Trust BM/AIDS
London WC1N 3XX
(071) 831 0330
which has a wide range of leaflets free
on request.

The Terrence Higgins Trust Helpline:
(071) 242 1010

National AIDS Helpline: (0800) 567123
Welsh AIDS campaign Helpline:
(0222) 223443

Northern Ireland AIDS line
Helpline: (0232) 326117
Scottish AIDS Monitor
Helpline: (031) 557 1757

Positively Women
333 Gray's Inn Road
London WC1 8PX
(071) 837 9705
A support group for women who are HIV
positive.

London Lesbian and Gay Switchboard
(071) 837 7324
will discuss AIDS/HIV infection and put
you in touch with local support groups.

ALCOHOL ADDICTION
Alcoholics Anonymous
Look in phone book for your local group.
Al-Ateen and Al-Anon
England and Wales (071) 403 0888
Northern Ireland (0232) 243489

ALTERNATIVE THERAPY
Institute for Complementary Medicine
21 Portland Place
London W1N 3AF
(071) 636 9543

Society of Homeopaths
2 Artisan Road
Northampton
London NN1 4HU
(0604) 21400
*Your local library or health food shop may
have names of individual practitioners.*

ANOREXIA NERVOSA - see Eating
Disorders

BIRTH CONTROL -
see Contraception

BISEXUALITY - see Gay and Lesbian
Advice Organizations

CANCER
The Women's National Cancer Control
Campaign
Suna House
128 Curtain Road
London EC2 3AR
(071) 729 4658
*Provides information on early detection and
treatment.*

CONTRACEPTION
*For advice on contraception, pregnancy
counselling and abortion contact:*
British Pregnancy Advisory Service
(BPAS)
7 Belgrave Road
London SW1V 1QB
(071) 708 1234
*Also has centres in Birmingham, Bristol,
Burnley, Coventry, Edinburgh,
London, and Liverpool. Provides counselling
and advice on all aspects.*

Pregnancy Advisory Service
13 Charlotte Street
London W1P 1HD
(071) 637 8962
Counselling and advice on all aspects.

Brook Advisory Centres
233 Tottenham Court Road
London W1A 9AE
(071) 580 2991
*Provides counselling and advice and
information of nearest clinic for abortion.*

Family Planning Association
27 Mortimer Street
London W1N 7RJ
(071) 636 7866
*For your nearest FPA clinic, look the phone
book or contact the head office above.*

Irish Family Planning Association
15 Mountjoy Square
Dublin
Tel. Dublin 744133

COUNSELLING
*For sympathetic and impartial counselling on
personal, emotional, sexual, family and other
problems contact:*
British Association for Counselling
37a Sheep Street
Rugby
Warwickshire
CV21 3BX
(0788) 578328

MIND
22 Harley Street
London W1N 2ÈD
(071) 637 0741

The National Association of Young
Peoples' Counselling and Advisory
Service
17-23 Albion Street
Leicester LE1 6GD
(0533) 471200

Teenage Information Network (TIN)
102 Harper Road
London SE1 6AQ
(071) 403 2444 (London only)

CRUSE (for bereaved people)
126 Sheen Road
Richmond
Surrey TW9 1UR
(081) 940 4818

DEPRESSION AND DESPAIR
Contact the organizations listed above under
Counselling. If you feel desperate, ring the
Samaritans. You will find the local number in
the phone book or you can ask the operator to
put you through directly.

DISABILITY AND SEX
For advice and information contact:
S.P.O.D. (Sexual Problems of the
Disabled)
286 Camden Road
London N7 OBJ
(071) 607 8851

Outsiders' Club
Box 4ZB
London W1A 4ZB
(071) 499 0900
Social and campaigning group

The Disabled Living Foundation
380–384 Harrow Road
London W9 2HU
(071) 289 6111

RADAR (Royal Association for
Disability and Rehabilitation)
25 Mortimer Street
London W1N 8AB
(071) 637 5400

DRUGS
For help with a drugs problem contact:
Standing Conference on Drug Abuse
(SCODA)
1–4 Hatton Place
Hatton Garden
London EC1N 8ND

Community Drug Project
30 Manor Place
London SE17 3BB
(071) 703 0559

Tranx
Helpline: (0860) 651133
For tranquillizer addiction
Phoenix House
1 Elliot Bank
Forest Hill
London SE23
(081) 699 5478
Residential drug rehabilitation project

EATING DISORDERS

Eating Disorders Association
The Priory Centre
11 Priory Road
High Wycombe
Bucks HP13 6SL
(0494) 21431
It has a network of self-help groups and provides support for those with anorexia and bulimia.

GAY AND LESBIAN ADVICE ORGANIZATION

For information and advice on being gay, lesbian or bisexual contact:
Lesbian and Gay Switchboard
BM Switchboard
London
WC1N 3XX
(071) 837 7324
24 hour telephone help service on practical and emotional problems affecting gays and lesbians.

Scottish Gay Switchboard
PO Box 169
Edinburgh EH1 3UU
Tel: (031) 556 4049

Lesbian and Gay Youth Movement
PO Box BMGYM
London WC1N 3XX
(081) 317 9690

Lesbian and Gay Black Group
BM Box 4390
London WC1N 3XX
Send SAE for details of your local group

London Lesbian and Gay Centre
69 Cowcross Street
London EC1M 6BP

London Bisexual Group
BM Bi
London WC1N 3XX
(081) 569 7500

Parents of lesbian and gay children might want to contact:

Parents Anonymous
(081) 668 4805 (24 hrs)

HERPES

For help and advice for people with herpes:
The Herpes Association
41 North Road
London N7
(071) 609 9061

HIV INFECTION - see AIDS

INCEST/ABUSE OF CARE

The following organizations will be able to give you confidential advice and find you a place of safety if necessary:

Childline
Freepost 1111
London EC4B 4BB (no stamp needed)
Freephone (0800) 1111 (no charge)
24 hour service for children and young people in danger or in trouble

Incest Crisis Line
32 Newbury Close
Northolt
Middlesex UB5 4JF
This service is run by incest survivors:
Shirley (081) 890 4732
Kate (081) 593 9428
Choices (for people in the Cambridge area) (0223) 314438

LEGAL RIGHTS
The Children's Legal Centre
20 Compton Terrace
London N1 2UN
(071) 359 6251

Release
169 Commercial Street
London E1 6BW
Emergency (24 hrs): (071) 603 8654

Campaign for Homosexual Equality (CHE)
Room 221
38 Mount Pleasant
London WC1 OAT
(071) 833 3912

National Council for Civil Liberties
21 Tabard Street
London SE1 4LA
(071) 403 3888
Campaigning organization on wide range of civil rights

PREGNANCY - see also Contraception
For advice if you keep the baby:

National Council For One Parent Families
255 Kentish Town Road
London NW5 2LX
(071) 267 1361

Scottish Council For Single Parents
23 Castle Street
Edinburgh
EH2 3DN
(031) 220 0929

Gingerbread
35 Wellington Street
London WC2E 7BN
(071) 240 0953

Maternity Alliance
15 Britannia Street
London WC1X 9JP
(071) 837 1265
Advice on rights and benefits during pregnancy and after the birth.

For advice on fostering and adoption contact:

National Foster Care Association
Francis House
Francis Street
London SW1P 1DE
(071) 828 6266

Parent To Parent Information On Adoption Society
Lower Boddington
Daventry
Northants NN11 6YB
(0327) 60295

PROSTITUTION
At the time of writing there is only one organization which specializes in helping young people involved in prostitution:

Streetwise
Springside House
84 Northend Road
London W14
(071) 373 8860

RAPE/ASSAULT

For girls and women:
The Rape Crisis Centre (also for incest
survivors)
PO Box 69
London WC1X 9NJ
(071) 837 1600 (24 hrs)
Liverpool
(021) 233 2122 (24hrs)
*The number of your nearest Rape Crisis
Centre should be in the phone book.*

Women's Aid
52-54 Featherstone Street
London
EC1Y 8RT
(071) 251 6537
*Will give you details of your nearest women's
refuge*

*For boys and men who have been raped or
assaulted:*
Survivors
38 Mount Pleasant
London WC1 OAP
(071) 833 3737 Tuesday, Wednesday,
Thursday and Sunday.

SCHIZOPHRENIA

National Schizophrenia Fellowship
79 Victoria Road
Surbiton
Surrey KT6 4NS
(081) 547 3937

SMOKING

For advice on quitting smoking contact:
ASH (Action on Smoking and Health)
5-11 Mortimer Street
London W1N 7RH
(071) 637 9843/6

WOMEN

The London Women's Centre
Wesley House
4 Wild Court
London
WC2B 5AU
(071) 831 6946
*Gives information about women's groups,
meetings and campaigns in your area.*

IN CANADA

Planned Parenthood Federation of
Canada
1 Nicholas Street Suite 430
Ottawa, Ontario
KIN 7B7
613 238 4474

Institute for the Prevention of
Child Abuse
25 Spadina Road
Toronto, Ontario
M5R 2S9
416 965 1900

Kids Help Phoneline
(national free phone)
1 800 668 6868
*This will give information on local rape and
sexual abuse services as well as other agencies.*

IN NEW ZEALAND
Family Planning Association
214 Karangahape Road
Auckland 1
09 796 182

Help Foundation
(for sexual assault victims)
1st floor, 427 Queen Street
Auckland 1
09 764 404

Child Abuse Prevention Society
Almorah Road
Epsom
Auckland 3
09 601 052

Rape Crisis
63 Ponsonby Road
Auckland 2
09 764 404

IN AUSTRALIA
Child Protection and Family Crisis
02 818 5555 (24 hours)
Crisis Care
Brisbane 07 224 6855
Adelaide 08 272 1222
Perth 09 321 4144 or free phone
008 199 008
*Family planning and rape crisis services can be
contacted through local directory.*